Author and Editor
Carol Field Dahlstrom

Book Design
Lyne Neymeyer

Photography: Dean Tanner— Primary Image
Copy Editing: Janet Figg, Jill Philby
Proofreading: Elizabeth Dahlstrom
Food Artist: Jennifer Peterson
Props and Location: Roger Dahlstrom
Technical Assistant: Judy Bailey
How-to Illustrations: Kristen Krumhardt
Recipe Development and Testing: Elizabeth Dahlstrom, Ardith Field, Barbara Hoover, Jennifer Peterson

Special thanks to these people for helping to make some of the items in the book:
Donna Chesnut, Kristin Detrick, Ardith Field, Barbara Hoover,
Janet Petersma, Jennifer Peterson, Ann E. Smith, Jan Temeyer

ISBN 978-0-9768446-6-2
Library of Congress Control Number: 2007903167
Copyright © Carol Field Dahlstrom, Inc. 2007

Separations: Integrity Printing, Des Moines, Iowa
Printed in the United States of America
First Edition

ABOUT THE AUTHOR

Carol Field Dahlstrom has produced over 90 best-selling crafts, food, decorating, children's, and
holiday books for Better Homes and Gardens®, Bookspan®, and her own publishing company,
Brave Ink Press. She has made numerous television, radio, and speaking appearances sharing her
books and encouraging simple and productive ways to spend family time together. Her creative
vision and experience make her books fun as well as informative. She lives with her family in the
country near Des Moines, Iowa, where she writes and designs from her studio.

Carol Field Dahlstrom, Inc. and Brave Ink Press strive to provide high quality products and information that will make
your life happier and more beautiful. Please write or e-mail us with your comments, questions, and suggestions or to
inquire about purchasing books at braveink@aol.com or Brave Ink Press, P.O. Box 663, Ankeny, Iowa 50021.

Visit us at www.braveink.com to see upcoming books from
Brave Ink Press or to purchase books.

The "I can do that!" books™

Carol Field Dahlstrom

Merry *Christmas* Ideas

225
**projects for
crafting, cookie-baking,
gift-giving, decorating,
and memory-making**

Carol Field Dahlstrom, Inc.

Brave Ink Press

Ankeny, Iowa

Time to Enjoy the Season

You love Christmas more than any other holiday—but you are busy. You are really busy. First, there are the stores encouraging you to start decorating even before Thanksgiving. Then, there are the parties to plan, the programs to attend, the cards to write, and the packages to wrap. You want to go shopping with your mother and the kids want to go see Santa. Your heart is in the right place, but your feet just can't move fast enough.

You love Christmas and you want to make this Christmas meaningful and wonderful for your family and friends. You want to create special gifts, decorate your home, and make yummy treats that they'll remember for ever. But you also want time to enjoy the season. Some days you wonder if you can do it all.

Because you love Christmas, we have given you all kinds of ideas that really take very little time. Try making easy beaded necklaces or simple paper ornaments. Wrap those gifts with a simple bow and candy cane or put clever little gifts in decorated canning jars. If you love to sew, recycle those old sweaters into beautiful felted-wool bags. Use beautiful scrapbook papers and purchased stickers to make simple greeting cards and gift tags. Stack simple shaped cut-out cookies frosted in holiday colors. You'll find over 225 easy ideas to make your holiday special— with time to spare.

You love Christmas. So take a breath. Look around you. The spirit of the season is everywhere and now you'll have time to enjoy it all. With the ideas and projects in this book, you'll be saying "I can do that!" Merry Christmas!

Carol Field Dahlstrom

Contents

ornaments

easy

handmade

playful

& trims

sparkling

clever

Heavenly Angels

Add some heavenly sparkle to your holiday by creating a host of angels made from golden wire. Dress the little angels with pretty bows and hang them on the tree or use them as delightful package trims. Step-by-step instructions are on page 20.

Quick Wrap

Create a beautiful package wrap in no time using plain-colored paper and two different widths of ribbon. Simply wrap the gift and then use crafts glue to adhere the ribbon to the box. Use pieces of double-sided tape to adhere the sweet angels.

Happy Paper Trims

Fill a tree with bright trims made from scrapbook papers. Whether you choose to make Pretty Poinsettias, Christmas Flowers, Paper Spheres, or Playful Pinwheels, you'll have fun creating these magical shapes. Instructions and full-size patterns are on page 21.

Silver Stars

Silver pipe cleaners formed around star cookie cutters make so-easy trims that everyone in the family will want to create. Add a little red jingle bell to complete the holiday look. Instructions are on page 22.

Snowman Pair

Purchased clear ornaments become playful snowmen in no time with just a little paint and scraps of trims to give them personality-plus. Paint the snowmen using transparent glass paints and then glue on ribbons or beads to create winter attire. Fill the ornaments with purchased loose snow to make the smiles show even more. Instructions are on page 22.

Partridge in a Pear Tree

Folded lightweight paper is easily cut into a Paper Partridge Garland in no time. Transform artificial pears into Tiny Pear Bird Perches to add to the tree. Add fresh-sliced citrus to make this a stunning holiday display. Instructions are on page 23.

Crafter's Secret

When making folded paper garlands, always use strong but lightweight paper and sharp scissors to get a clean and crisp edge. Practice first by folding the paper to see how many thicknesses the scissors can easily cut before starting the final project.

Paisley Cookie Trims

Decorate your favorite roll-out cookie in a pretty paisley design. The dots and swirls are surprisingly easy to create and no two are alike. Make cookies to hang on the tree—but be sure to make enough to eat as well. The recipe is on page 86 and ornament tips are on page 24.

Cookie Purse Ornaments

Pretty purses and bags are fun all times of the year—so decorate this roll-out cookie variety with designer-style confidence. Add ribbons to the handles to hang them on the tree. The recipe is on page 88 and ornament tips are on page 24.

15

Printed-Paper Snowmen

Pick your favorite scrapbook papers and colorful brads to make some well-dressed snowmen. Combine them with some Sparkling Mittens to create a snow-filled holiday tree. Instructions and full-size patterns are on page 27.

Sparkling Mittens

Create mittens that you can hang on the Christmas tree using a simple homemade clay recipe. Use cookie cutters to cut the shapes that you like and add glitter to the cut-out ornaments for extra sparkle. Use a piece of shiny white ribbon to hang the trim on the tree. Instructions are on page 25.

Good Idea

When making any kind of craft clay or dough, always mark the container or bag where the product is kept with a "do not eat" marking. Oftentimes craft dough and food products can look alike, so mark the container to avoid any confusion.

Seeing Pink Ornaments

Make pink the theme for creating a special pastel tree. The Pink Daisy Trim uses bits of paper and pretty ribbon to resemble a fresh daisy. The Peppermint Ice Cream Ornament gets inspiration from a sweet scoop of ice cream, and the Beaded in Pink Trim lines up all shapes of beads to make a dressed-up look. Instructions are on page 28.

Heavenly Angels
Shown on page 8

What you need (for one angel)
24-gauge wire cut into the following lengths: 30 inches for wings, 44 inches for head/body, 20 inches for halo and hanger
4 small round beads
5 inches of ¼-inch-wide ribbon
Crafts glue

What you do
• **For wings:** Wrap the 30-inch piece of wire around four fingers 3-4 times to form a loop. Twist in the middle (see photo A). Set aside.
• **For head/body:** Using the 44-inch piece of wire, wrap around thumb and twist at base to secure end (head). Wrap long loose end in a continuous crazy eight shape around 4 fingers to form the skirt. Continue to loop over thumb (head) and around the fingers (skirt), 3 times or until the entire length of the wire is used. Twist the end of the wire at the intersection of the two shapes to secure the end. Use fingers to mold and flatten out wire at the base of the larger bottom section to make skirt (see photo B). Set aside.
• **For halo and hanger:** Using the 20-inch piece of wire, about 4 inches from cut end, form halo by wrapping wire loosely around thumb to make circle. Twist wire at start of circle to finish halo and continue twisting down the straight 4-inch tail that started this piece. Loop long straight end up and over halo in a circle to form hanger. Twist at bottom (see photo C).

• **To attach 3 sections:** Place the wings behind the head/body section at the twisted intersections. Hold the halo piece behind the wings and body sections. Take the remaining straight wire from this halo piece and wrap it around and over in a crisscross fashion at the intersection of both the wings and the main body pieces, threading the wire through the body and over to the back around the wings, then up through the body section again several times, pulling tightly, to anchor the pieces together. Twist the end at the back of the middle intersection to complete. Decorate the angel by tying a small bow and gluing over the center intersection. Glue small beads to halo, wings, and/or bottom skirt, if desired.

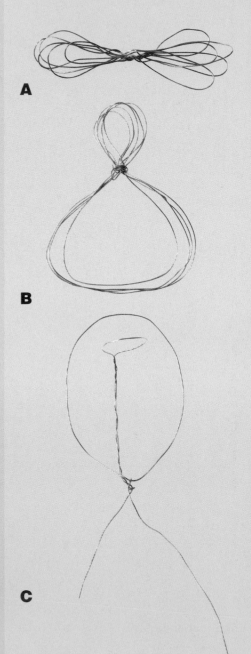

A

B

C

20

Happy Paper Trims
Shown on page 9

What you need
Tracing paper or copier
Lightweight cardboard
Decorative two-sided papers such as scrapbooking paper
Small colored mini brads; ribbon or string for hanging; scissors

What you do
• **For the Pretty Poinsettia:** Copy or trace the pattern, right. Draw around the pattern on the lightweight cardboard to make a template. Cut out. For each flower, trace petal template onto red or white decorative paper five times. Cut out shapes. Fold shapes in half, folding some at slanted, irregular angles. Overlap pieces, holding them together in the center. With awl point, make small hole in center at several places and insert brads. Tie length of string behind flower or glue ribbon to back to hang.

• **For the Paper Sphere:** Copy or trace the pattern, right. Draw around the pattern on the lightweight cardboard to make a template. Cut out. For each ornament, trace sphere template onto double sided decorative paper five times. Cut out shapes. Stack pieces and make a small hole in both ends with the sharp point of an awl. Insert a colored brad into holes of one end of all five shapes. Fan pieces out and insert a second brad through holes of opposite ends. Work shapes around to form a sphere. Tie length of string underneath brad or glue ribbon to back to hang.

• **For the Christmas Flower:** Copy or trace the pattern, right. Draw around the pattern on the lightweight cardboard to make a template. Cut out. For each flower, trace paper sphere template onto decorative paper five times. Cut out shapes. Softly fold shapes in half. With pointed ends of one shape together, make small hole in ends with awl. Poke decorative brad through one petal and overlap with other petals one by one, poking brad through centers. Fan shapes out. Make 2-4 cuts from fold to center of each petal. Gently bend up alternating cuts to fluff out shape. Attach string or glue ribbon to back to hang.

• **For the Playful Pinwheel:** Enlarge and copy or trace the pattern, bottom right. Draw around the pattern on the lightweight cardboard to make a template. Cut out. Trace around pinwheel template onto two-sided decorative paper. Mark diagonal lines from corners in toward center, stopping about ½-inch from center mark. Cut out shape and slit along diagonal lines. With awl point, make small holes through paper at points marked on pattern. Bring corners with holes to center hole and insert decorative brad through all holes. Attach string or glue ribbon to back for hanging.

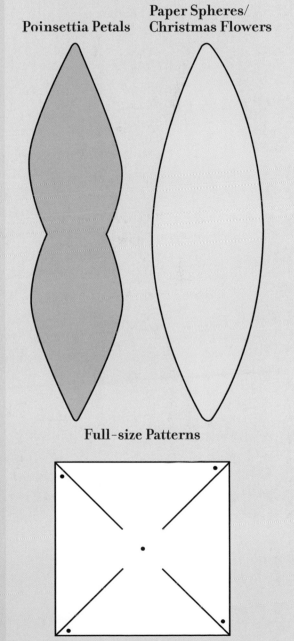

Poinsettia Petals **Paper Spheres/Christmas Flowers**

Full-size Patterns

Playful Pinwheel Pattern
enlarge 200%

Silver Stars
Shown on page 10

What you need
Small star-shaped cookie cutter
Silver pipe cleaner; scissors
Small purchased red ornament
Small piece of 24-gauge wire

What you do
Lay the cookie cutter on a flat surface. Wrap the pipe cleaner around the cookie cutter pressing the pipe cleaner into the shape of the cookie cutter. Carefully remove the pipe cleaner and twist the top together. Cut off any excess pipe cleaner using scissors. Wire the small red ornament into the top center of the star.

Snowman Pair
Shown on page 11

What you need
Two purchased round glass ornaments with removable tops and flat fronts (available at craft stores)
Rubber band
Transparent glass paints in black, orange, red, and green
Two foam brushes; disposable plate
Small paint brush
Loose white snow flakes (available in bags at crafts stores)
Scrap of ribbon and beaded trim
Crafts glue suitable for glass

What you do
Be sure the ornament is clean and dry. Wrap the rubber band around each ornament about one third down from the top. Following the manufacturer's directions for the use of the paint, use the foam brush to paint the top third of the ornaments starting at the rubber band. Paint one ornament red and one green. See Photo A. Let the paint dry. Remove the rubber bands. Use the crafts glue to glue the trim around bottom of the painted area. Let dry. Cut a small V-shaped piece of foam from the other paint brush. Place a little orange paint on the disposable plate. Dip the V-shaped piece into the paint and print the nose on each ornament front. Let dry. Use the small paint brush to paint the eyes and mouth. Let dry. Take the top off of the ornament and fill half full with loose snow. Replace top on ornament.

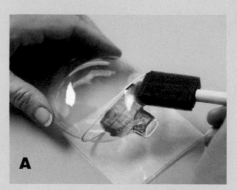

A

Paper Partridge Garland

Shown on pages 12–13

What you need

Tracing paper or copier
3 ½ x 24-inch strip of lightweight paper
    in desired color
Pencil
Scissors
Paper punch
Crafts glue

What you do

Trace or copy the patterns, right. Set the wing pattern aside. Fold the strip of lightweight paper accordian-style every 3 ½ inches. Transfer the pattern to the folded paper being sure that the edges of the paper are on the fold. Cut out. Use the paper punch to make a hole for the eyes. Fold the edge of the wing and glue in place as indicated on the pattern. Allow to dry.

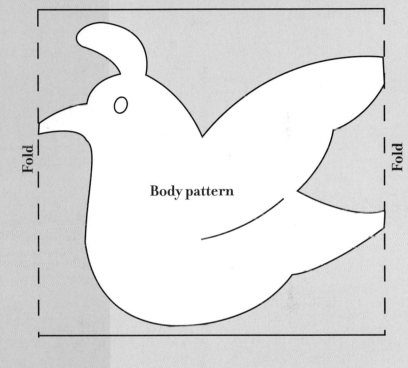

Fold   Fold

Body pattern

Tiny Pear Bird Perches

Shown on page 12–13

What you need

Small purchased acrylic pears
    (available at craft stores)
Drill and drill bit
Sphagnum moss
Toothpick

What you do

Use the drill and bit to make a hole in the front of the pear. Cut or break the toothpick in half. Push into the pear above the hole. Fill the hole with a tiny pinch of sphagnum moss. Hang on the tree.

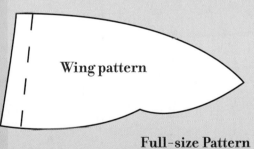

Wing pattern

Full-size Pattern

23

Paisley Cookie Trims

Shown on page 14

What you need

One recipe Pretty Paisley Cookies (see page 86)
Paisley cookie cutter set (see Sources, page 159)
One recipe Meringue Icing (see page 87)
Food coloring
Small drinking straw
¼-inch-wide ribbon in desired colors

What you do

Make the cookies as directed on page 86. Before baking, make a hole in the top of the cookie using a drinking straw. Decorate as directed. Place ribbon in the hole of the cookie and hang on the tree.

Cookie Purse Ornaments

Shown on page 15

What you need

One recipe Fancy Purse Cookies (see page 88)
Purse cookie cutter (see Sources, page 159)
One recipe Meringue Icing (see page 87)
Food coloring
Desired cookie embellishments (see Sources, page 159)
¼-inch-wide ribbon in desired colors

What you do

Make the cookies as directed on page 88. Decorate with Meringue Icing using ideas and tips on page 88. Place a ribbon in the space in the purse handle and tie a knot. Use the other ends of the ribbon to tie the cookie on the tree.

Sparkling Mittens
Shown on pages 16–17

What you need

1 cup granulated sugar
3 tablespoons white glue
1 tablespoon glitter
1 teaspoon water
Round toothpick
Paring knife
Waxed paper
Rolling pin
Cookie cutters
Small lengths metallic thread, nylon thread, or narrow cording

What you do

Mix sugar, glue, glitter and water in small bowl. Lay a square of waxed paper on counter and flatten the ball of crystal dough with hands. Lay another square of waxed paper on top. Gently roll out the dough with a rolling pin to approximately a ¼-inch thickness, keeping the dough between the waxed paper. Remove the waxed paper and cut out desired shapes using cookie cutters. Set aside. Re-roll remaining dough, as needed.

Use a round toothpick that has been cut in half to make a hole at the top of the shape for hanging. Use the edge of a paring knife to smooth out and pat together the edges of the shapes, as needed. Lay shapes out on clean waxed paper to dry overnight. Turn over and dry other side.

Note: This dough is craft dough only and should never be eaten.

Special Tip

When packing away fragile, flat, handmade, Christmas ornaments at the end of the holiday season, purchase plastic containers that are not too deep. Start with a layer of bubble wrap at the bottom. Lay the ornaments on the bubble wrap and place cut piece of paper towel rolls beside the ornaments to serve as spacers between layers. This will keep the weight off of the fragile pieces.

Printed-Paper Snowman
Shown on page 16

What you need (for one snowman)
Tracing paper or copier
Pencil
4 x 6-inch piece of white tone-on-tone cardstock paper
Scrap of black cardstock paper
Scrap of printed colored cardstock paper
Scissors
Crafts glue
Small brads in black, orange, and desired colors
Narrow ribbon

What you do
Copy the snowmen patterns, opposite, onto tracing paper. Cut out.
Trace around the main snowman piece onto the white cardstock
paper. Cut out. Trace around the scarf pattern onto the colored
paper. Cut out. Make cuts along the end for the scarf fringe.

   Choose a hat pattern and trace around on black paper. Cut out.
Use crafts glue to glue the pieces in place. Use black brads for the
eyes and mouth. Place an orange brad in backwards for the nose. Use
desired color brads for the buttons.

   Punch a hole in the top and hang on the tree using narrow ribbon.

Special Tip

There are a variety of wonderful scrapbooking
papers available at crafts, discount, and
scrapbooking stores. Some printed papers can be
found in heavier weight cardstock and some are
on lighter weight paper. Choose heavier weight
cardstock for ornaments and greeting cards. Choose
lighter weight papers for gluing to scrapbook pages
and for cutting garlands.

Hat pattern option 1

Hat pattern option 2

Hat pattern option 3

Snowman body pattern

Scarf pattern

Full-size patterns

Seeing Pink Ornaments

Shown on pages 18–19

What you need **for the Peppermint Ice Cream Ornament**
Purchased pink matte-finish ornament
Gesso (a paint sealer available at art and craft stores)
Two drinking glasses
Bamboo stick; paintbrush
Red glass paint; white glitter

What you do **for the Peppermint Ice Cream Ornament**
Use the knife to spread the gesso on the ornament. While it is wet, brush some glass paint onto the gesso. The paint will run into the gesso. Secure the ornament by placing the bamboo stick in the ornament top and balancing the stick between the two glasses. As it dries, rotate the ornament to achieve the peppermint effect. Dust with glitter before the ornament is completely dry.

What you need **for the Pink Daisy Trim**
Purchased pink matte-finish ornament
Small pieces of pink paper
Small piece of pink ribbon
Fine pink glitter; crafts glue

Full-size petal pattern

What you do **for the Pink Daisy Trim**
Trace the petal pattern, above, and cut out. Trace around the petal five times onto the pink scrapbook paper. Cut out. Bend the petal at the top and glue to the top of the ornament. Glue the ribbon around the center of the ornament. Add dots of glue on top of the ribbon and on the paper petals. Dust with glitter. Let dry.

What you need **for the Beaded in Pink Trim**
Purchased pink matte-finish ornament
Assorted seed and bugle beads
8-inch piece of 24-gauge wire
Crafts glue; tweezers

What you do **for the Beaded in Pink Trim**
Use the crafts glue to make a line of glue from the top to the bottom of the ornament. Use the tweezers to place the beads in a random line. Repeat all around the ornament allowing the glue and beads to dry on one side before moving to the next side. String some beads on the wire for a hanger, securing the ends.

more ideas

Start a tradition by giving a handmade ornament as a gift to a special person each year. Place the ornament in a square box and wrap in plain-colored paper. Write "starting a new tradition" over and over on the outside of the wrapped box using a gold marking pen. Add a pretty bow to the package.

❦

Put ornaments of all the same hue in a large crystal glass bowl. Display in the center of the table resting on a favorite scrapbook paper or holiday napkin.

❦

Use narrow holiday ribbons instead of ornament hangers to hang the trims on the Christmas tree this year.

❦

Make copies of favorite photos, cut out, and glue to a star-shaped piece of scrapbook paper for a simple "from the kids" gift.

❦

When giving an ornament as a gift, make a special hanger by stringing beads onto colored wire and attaching it to the ornament.

❦

Fill small florist bags with goodies and hang them on the tree as holiday ornaments.

❦

Use a baby stocking as a gift-holder for money for a first Christmas.

❦

Display favorite round ornaments propped in crystal candlestick holders. Group on a mantel or buffet for a striking effect.

❦

Spray-paint tiny purchased grapevine wreaths with your favorite holiday color. Glue miniature trims to the wreaths and hang on the Christmas tree.

For your banister this year, use a fruit theme. Attach fresh or artificial greens to the banister and then wire fruit-shaped or fruit-colored ornaments to the greens. Add curls of real orange, lime, and lemon rind to finish the look and to add a fruity aroma.

❦

Purchase monogram letters that spell the words "Noel" or "Joy". Glue each monogram letter to a piece of colored felt and frame each one in a small gold or silver frame. Tie the little frames on the tree.

❦

As you trim the tree, take turns telling favorite Christmas memories. Let the little ones tell about their favorite Christmas as Grandma and Grandpa share their memories.

❦

The little ones can make quick kiddie garlands by stringing candies and cereals together. Using green waxed dental floss, string candies and cereals with holes such as fruity cereals, candy savers, gummy candies, and oat cereals. Tie the ends in a loop to keep the goodies from falling off.

❦

Add fresh greens or holly to unexpected places in your home. Tuck them under centerpieces, on windowsills, around picture frames, and on top of cupboards to add a festive holiday touch. Fresh holly is poisonous if eaten, so do not use near any food items.

❦

Use vintage handkerchiefs as delicate trims for your tree. Press the hankies into fan shapes and tie the top together with a fine ribbon. Tie on the tree.

wreaths, stockings & centerpieces

welcoming

elegant

festive

beautiful

stylish

Lines and Dots Quilted Mat

The colors of the season take on a playful look when they are quilted into a clever mantel or table mat. Machine quilting this project makes it quick and easy to make. Instructions are on page 48.

Crafter's Secret

When deciding on random placement of appliqué pieces, lay pieces of paper in the shape of the appliqué onto the fabric first. Adjust the position and then mark the final placement with a tailor's pencil.

Lines and Dots Quilted Stocking

Santa will love to fill this happy quilted stocking constructed in no time with strip piecing. The playful circles are added with machine appliqué. Instructions and patterns are on pages 48–49.

Striped Candy Centerpiece

Make a centerpiece in just the nick of time using wrapped candies, striped candy canes, a single white candle, and a pretty glass container. Instructions are on page 50.

Stamped Ice-Skate Wreath

A pair of white ice skates become the center of attention when they are rubber-stamped with a purchased snowflake stamp and hung in the middle of a pretty green wreath. Add some jingle bells to create a happy sound as guests come to call. Instructions are on page 50.

Fancy Flowers Wreath

Pretty purchased hot-pink flowers are arranged on a plastic foam wreath with just the right amount of shiny and colorful Christmas balls creating a stunning wreath. The wreath can be made in any color that matches your holiday theme. Instructions are on page 51.

Good Idea

Wreaths are usually hung on doors or in hallways, but they also make wonderful centerpieces. Just lay the wreath on a plate or tray and add a candle or tumbler of ornaments in the center of the wreath.

Festive Goblet Centerpiece

Find your favorite clear-glass goblets and fill
them with purchased ornaments and sprigs
of fresh greenery. Group them in the center
of the table to create a colorful centerpiece
that says "Merry Christmas!" Instructions
are on page 51.

Fabric Tree Trio

Cleverly constructed using printed batik-like green fabric and iron-on interfacing, this little forest of 3-D trees is easy and fun to make. Touches of glitter on the tree edges add a little holiday sparkle. Make a set for yourself or for a holiday gift. Instructions and patterns are on page 52–53.

Crafter's Secret

When adding glitter to any craft project, always place two pieces of waxed paper under the project. After dusting with glitter, pick up the top piece and set the glitter container on the remaining piece of paper before trying to put the glitter back in the container. The extra piece of paper will catch any spills.

Countertop Collections

Clear jars can be filled and grouped to make wonderful table arrangements or counter centerpieces for the holidays. Simply fill the jars with vintage cookbooks, cookie cutters, tassie tins, or any other favorite collection. For instructions and ideas for filling the jars, see page 56.

Colorful Retro-Look Stockings

Use brightly-colored, throwaway sweaters to make stockings that resemble those that hung on mantels decades ago. The softness of the sweater fabric mimics the retro-holiday look. Instructions and patterns are on pages 54—55.

Jingle Bells Presentation

Simple jingle bells can be collected and viewed under a cake or cheese dome to make a stunningly simple centerpiece. Instructions are on page 56.

Pretty Place Setting

Add your own bit of color and texture to an already beautifully shaped artifical pear by matching the leaf to the cloth napkin that you make. Instructions and pattern are on page 57.

Bows of Gold Centerpiece

Center a tall goblet in a clear glass bowl and fill with purchased gold bows. Add gold wrapped candies to the center goblet to complete the pretty centerpiece. Instructions are on page 60.

Vintage Jeweled Ball

Vintage jewelry takes on new shine when it is grouped on a round plastic foam ball. Display the lovely piece in a purchased gazing-ball stand for all to enjoy. Instructions are on page 60.

Pretty Holiday Napkins

Fold those pretty cloth napkins in all kinds of
interesting shapes in very little time. Add a take-
home table favor to the folded napkin to set the
table in style. Instructions and diagrams are on
page 58—59.

Good Idea

Shop after Christmas sales to find an
assortment of cloth napkins to have on
hand for holiday entertaining. If you
are having a large party and don't have
enough napkins of the same kind, use
three different styles and fold them all
in the same way.

Lines and Dots Stocking and Table Mat

Shown on pages 32—33

What you need for both stocking and mat
Tracing paper
Pencil; scissors
¼ yard each red, green, purple, and yellow cotton fabrics
⅓ yard striped cotton fabric for lining
Matching threads
⅓ yard thin quilt batting
Small pieces polyfil or cotton balls
Fusible webbing
20 x 20-inch square of thin cotton batting

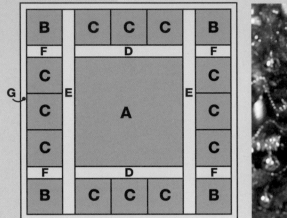

What you do

• For the Lines and Dots Stocking
Enlarge and trace the stocking pattern, opposite. Dots are full-size. Cut two stocking pattern pieces from lining fabric. Set aside. Cut 18-inch long strips of solid fabrics varying widths ranging from 1-2½ inches wide. Piece together solid fabrics to make a 18 x 24-inch piece of fabric. Cut two stocking patterns from this pieced fabric. Cut two stocking patterns from batting and baste to both stocking pieces.

• For Circle Embellishments: Trace circle patterns onto fusible webbing. Iron onto back of striped and yellow fabrics. Cut out circles along lines. Arrange as desired on striped pieced stocking pieces, overlapping some circles and leaving others separate. Iron down all yellow circle shapes and buttonhole stitch around edges using matching thread. Place striped dots where desired. Before ironing striped dots to stocking, insert a small balled up piece of polyfil or piece of cotton ball underneath striped circle shapes to give them more dimension. Lightly iron around outside edges. Buttonhole stitch around outside edges.

   With right sides together, sew stocking pieces together using ¼-inch seam allowance. Clip curves, turn and press lightly. With right sides together, sew lining pieces together. Clip curves. Iron top edges of stocking ½ inch to the inside and iron top edge of lining ½ inch to the outside. Insert lining inside the stocking. Make a hanging loop by cutting a 2 x 9-inch piece of striped fabric. With right sides together, stitch long edges together using a ¼-inch seam. Turn right side out and press. Insert loop at top right side of stocking between outside and lining fabrics. Baste together close to top folds. Stitch lining and stocking together by stitching close to top fold, also stitching through loop at side edge.

What you do

• For the Stripes and Dots Table Mat
Refer to the diagram, above, and cut the following:
• From the scraps of the striped pieced fabrics used to make the stocking, cut one square 9½ x 9½ inches (Piece A) and four squares 3½ x 3½ inches (Piece B).
• Cut 12 squares of fabric 3½ x 3½ inches from different striped fabrics (Piece C).
• For sashings, cut two 1½ x 9½ inch strips (Piece D), two strips 1½ x 17½ inches (Piece E), and four strips 1½ x 3½ inches (Piece F).
• For binding, cut 2¼-inch strips to equal about 78 inches total length. (Piece G).

• **Directions for Sewing:** Use ¼-inch seam allowances throughout. Sew D to opposite sides of A. Sew three C blocks together, four times. Sew one set of CCC to either side of AD. Stitch E pieces to both sides of ADCCC. Sew together two units of BFCCCFB and join to either side of center unit.

Use scraps of fabrics to piece together a backing to measure 19 x 19 inches. Layer top batting and backing, baste together and quilt as desired, or leave unquilted.

Trace three circle sizes onto fusible webbing paper. Iron onto desired fabrics and cut out shapes. Arrange on top of quilt top. Fuse in place only the shapes to lie underneath other overlapping circles and ones you wish to lie flat. Pin other overlapping circles on top other circles to determine overall look desired. Buttonhole stitch around flat shapes using matching threads. For striped circle shapes, place a small ball of cotton or polyfil underneath circle and fuse lightly around outside edges. Buttonhole stitch around outside edges. With wrong sides of long edges together, fold binding strip in half and iron flat. With right sides together, sew binding strip to outside edge of quilt top, fold to the back and tack in place.

Lines and Dots Stocking

Lengthwise grain

Enlarge 200%

1 ¾-inch

1 ⅛-inch

1 ¼-inch

Full-size Dot Patterns

Striped Candy Centerpiece
Shown on page 34

What you need
Clear glass candle holder
Small piece of floral sticky gum
White taper candle
Wrapped chocolate candies
Candy canes

What you do
Place a little piece of the floral gum in the bottom of the candleholder. Place the candle on the sticky gum. Arrange the candies around the candle. Carefully add the candy canes into the candies in a random fashion adjusting the canes to stay in place. Set the centerpiece on the table. Never leave a burning candle unattended.

Stamped Ice-Skate Wreath
Shown on page 35

What you need
White ice skates in a small size
Snowflake-motif rubber stamp
Red permanent ink stamp pad
Purchased artificial or real green 24-inch wreath
24-gauge wire; wire snips
Scissors
White garland
Red berry pokes
Red jingle bells
Purchased flat snowflake ornaments
1 yard of 2-inch-wide polka dot ribbon

What you do
Be sure the skates are clean and dry. Use the rubber stamp and the stamp pad to stamp snowflakes on the skates. Stamp one side at a time, drying one side before starting on another. Set aside to dry completely. Wrap the wreath with the white garland and secure with a little piece of wire. Wire in the berry pokes and flat snowflake ornaments. Wire the skates so they hang in the middle of the wreath. Wire the jingle bells at the top of the wreath. Tie the ribbon into a bow and wire to the top of the wreath. Add a wire hanger to the back of the wreath.

Fancy Flowers Wreath
Shown on page 36

What you need
12-inch plastic foam wreath such as Styrofoam
About 50 small purchased artificial flowers
Scissors
Small Christmas ornaments in similar colors as the flowers
White tacky crafts glue

What you do
If the artificial flowers have long stems, cut the stems to about ¾-inch long using the scissors.

Stick them into the foam wreath. Remove, add a dot of glue and put them back into the hole that was made. Repeat until the wreath is nearly covered. Add a dot of glue to the end of each small ornament and stick into the foam randomly, positioning the ornaments between the flowers. Allow to dry.

Festive Goblet Centerpiece
Shown on page 37

What you need
Clear glass goblets
Small purchased ornaments
Small pieces of fresh greenery
Wrapping paper to match or compliment ornament color

What you do
Be sure the goblets are clean and dry. Place the wrapping paper or other centerpiece paper or fabric under the glass, lining the glasses in a row in the center of the table. Add the ornaments and the greenery.

Fabric Tree Trio
Shown on pages 38

What you need
Tracing paper
Pencil
Scissors
⅜ yard lightweight cotton fabric
⅜ yard iron-on stabilizer such as Pellon brand Peltex #72
    double-sided fusible ultra firm stabilizer
Crafts glue
Glitter

What you do
Trace the patterns, right and opposite, using tracing paper or copier. Place that pattern on other folded piece of paper to make a full-size pattern for each tree shape. Set aside.

Sandwich stabilizer between wrong sides of fabric pieces. Fuse fabric to stabilizer. Place patterns onto fabric and draw around pattern edges, marking two pieces for each size of tree. Cut out shapes with sharp scissors. Make center slits in each tree shape, cutting the correct length ⅛-inch wide, as follows:

• **For small tree:** Center, measure, mark and cut a 2-inch long slit from the top of one tree. On another tree, make a 4-inch long slit from the bottom up.

• **For medium tree:** Center, measure, mark and cut a 2½-inch long slit from the top of one tree. On another tree, make a 4½-inch long slit from the bottom up.

• **For large tree:** Center, measure, mark and cut a 3-inch long slit from the top of one tree. On another tree, make a 5-inch long slit from the bottom up.

Spread a thin line of glue along outside top edges of tree. Sprinkle glitter over the glue to decorate and cover up the white edge left when cutting the stabilizer. Slide the tree with the bottom slit over the tree with the top slit. Embellish with garland, beads, and small ornaments if desired.

Fold

Small Tree Pattern

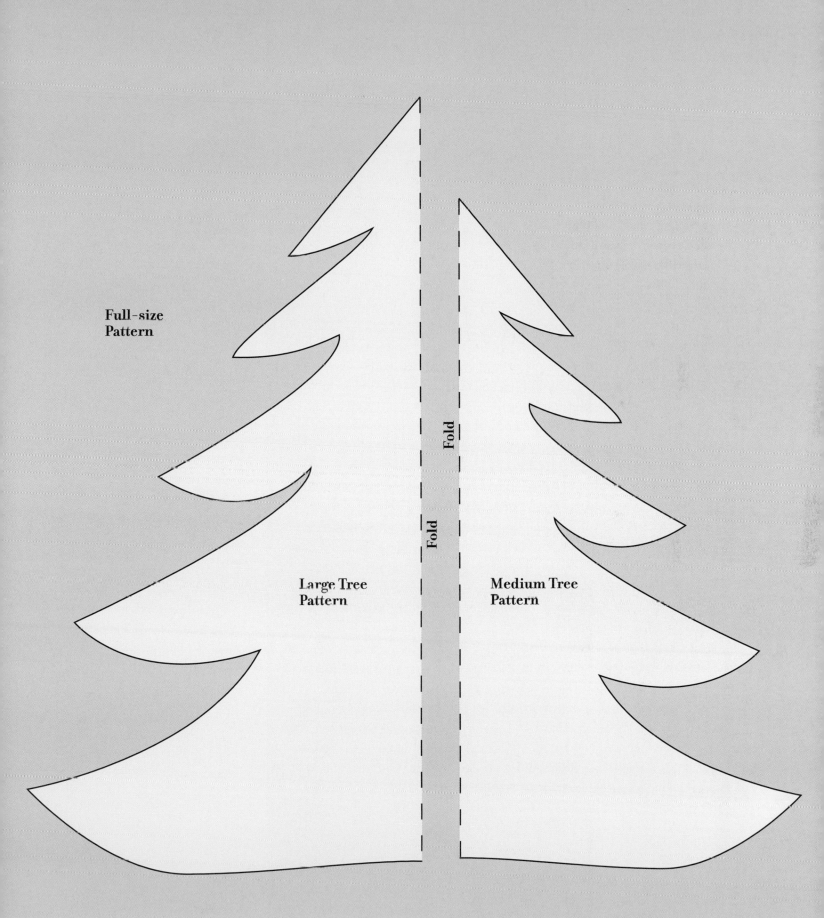

Full-size
Pattern

Fold

Fold

Large Tree
Pattern

Medium Tree
Pattern

53

Colorful Retro-Look Stockings

Shown on pages 40–41

What you need (for one stocking)
Tracing paper
Scissors; pencil
Old sweaters to cut up
Matching thread
¼ yard cotton fabric for lining
Vintage pin (optional)

What you do
Enlarge and trace or copy the pattern, opposite. Cut out.
With right sides together, cut 2 each of the stocking patterns from the sweater fabric and cotton lining fabric. Cut a 2 x 7-inch strip for the hanging loop and a 12x 6-inch long piece for the cuff from sweater fabric scraps.

With right sides together stitch around side edges of the stocking and lining pieces, leaving top edges open. Use a ¼-inch seam allowance for the linings and a ⅜-inch seam allowance for the sweater fabrics. (Hint: Because the sweater fabrics are so stretchy when cut, it is helpful to sew seams using an even feed foot on the sewing machine, reduce pressure on the presser foot, and lengthen the stitch to help stocking keep its shape.) Clip curves and turn sweater stocking pieces right side out. Insert lining inside stocking sweater piece, having wrong sides together and top edges even.

With right sides together, sew long edge of loop piece together. Turn right side out. With right sides together, sew short side of cuff piece to form a circular tube. Place hanging loop down inside stocking at side edge; overlap raw edges of ends at top edge of stocking. Baste through all layers of stocking, lining, and loop. Insert cuff inside stocking, with right side of cuff against the right side of the stocking lining. Sew around top edge through all layers, using a ⅜-inch seam allowance.

Flip cuff piece out over front of stocking, rolling cut edge underneath to form a 3½-inch wide finished cuff on the outside. Using thread to match the cuff, tack the cuff to the stocking by sewing a few stitches through both layers at the side seams. Add a vintage pin if desired.

Special Tip

When purchasing old sweaters to make craft projects, look carefully at the fabric content. If the sweater is to be used "as is" (as for these sweater stockings), be sure the sweater is tightly woven and will hold its shape well. If the sweater is to be "felted" (see tips, page 137), it is best to start with a sweater with a fiber content of at least 80% wool.

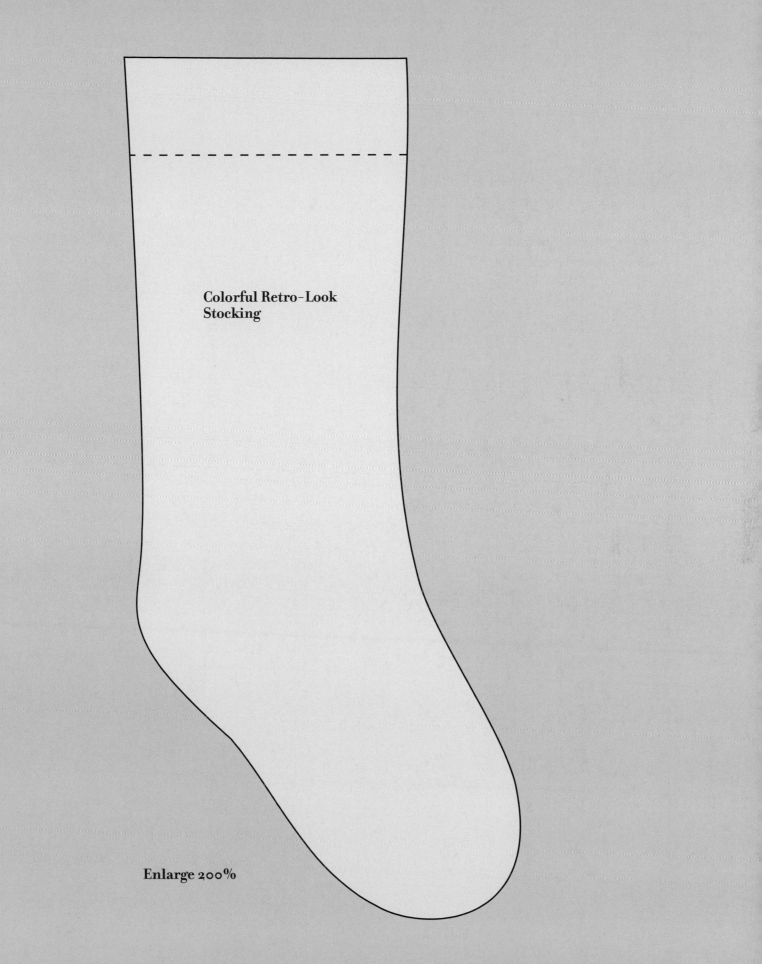

Colorful Retro-Look
Stocking

Enlarge 200%

Countertop Collections
Shown on page 41

What you need
Assortment of clear jars in varying sizes with lids
Collections of similar items to put in jars

What you do
Be sure the jars are clean and dry. Arrange the items in the jars with smaller flat pieces on the outside. If using cookie cutters, turn the cutters so different sides and edges are showing. Ideas for what to put in jars: Metal cookie cutters, red plastic cookie cutters, old cookbooks, tassie tins, large peppermint sticks, Christmas towels, yards of colored garlands, vintage kitchen tools.

Jingle Bells Presentation
Shown on page 42

What you need
Cake or cheese plate with clear dome top
Jingle bells in desired sizes and colors
Ribbon

What you do
Be sure the dome is clean and dry. Turn the dome upside down and fill with desired sizes and colors of jingle bells. Turn the plate upside down and place over the filled dome. Turn the entire plate and dome right side up. Add a ribbon if desired.

Pretty Place Setting

Shown on page 43

What you need (for four place settings)

Tracing paper
½ yard of printed 45-inch-wide fabric
Pencil
Scissors
Small pieces of fusible interfacing
4 purchased artificial pears
Four 1-inch pieces of 24-gauge wire
Iron

What you do

To make the napkins, cut four 11x11 inch squares from the fabric. Set the scraps aside for the pear leaves. Narrow hem the edges of each napkin and press.

To make the pear leaf, trace the full-size leaf pattern, below. Set aside. Fuse the interfacing between two pieces of the fabric scraps keeping wrong sides together. Trace around the leaf pattern four times onto the fused fabric. Cut out. Carefully open up the flat end of the leaf and insert the wire. Reiron the fabric together. Remove original leaf from the pear if necessary. Poke the wire that protrudes from the fabric leaf into the pear top. Arrange pear with napkin on the plate. Fold napkin and place on plate beside pear.

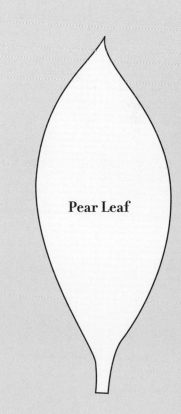

Pear Leaf

Full-size Pattern

Special Tip

When finding fabrics to make handmade cloth napkins, be sure and choose fabrics that are made of natural fibers such as 100% cotton or linen. Natural fibers absorb moisture well and will wash and iron nicely. Natural fibers also fold best into crisp folds that will hold their shape.

Pretty Holiday Napkins

Shown on pages 46–47

What you need

Square cloth napkins in desired color
Iron
Ribbon
Small Christmas item to tuck or tie onto folded napkin

What you do

Start with a clean and flat-pressed napkin. Choose the napkin fold that you wish to make and, referring to the diagrams, right and below, fold the napkin following the step-by-step illustrations. Tie or tuck the small Christmas item in or on the napkin or tie on with a ribbon and lay on the plate.

Special Tip

To make your holiday table even more festive, make name cards for everyone at the table. Fold a 2x3-inch rectangle of colorful scrapbook paper in half (the long way) and use alphabet stickers as monograms or spell out the entire name on the folded paper. Place the name card above the plate at each place setting.

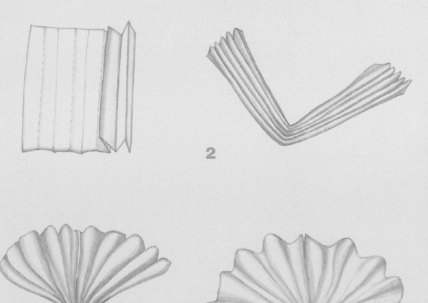

For the Fan Napkin, fold the napkin in half. Fold the napkin accordian-style starting from the short end (diagram 1). Fold the napkin in half again (diagram 2). Use a small piece of ribbon to tie a knot about 2-inches from the folded bottom (diagram 3). Tie on a small ornament if desired. Fan out the napkin top (diagram 4).

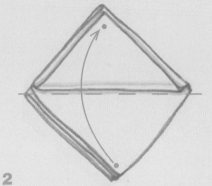

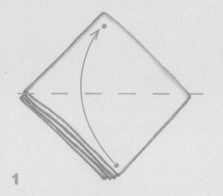

1

2

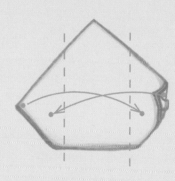

3

4

For the Royal Napkin, fold the napkin in half and in half again. Lay the napkin with the loose points at the bottom and bring up one layer almost to the top (diagram 1). Fold up another layer almost to the first layer (diagram 2). Continue folding until all the layers are folded up close to the previous layer.
Turn the folded napkin over and fold in the sides.
Tuck a candy cane in the napkin opening if desired.

1

2

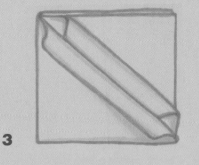

3

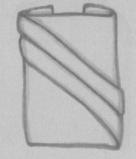

4

For the Rolled Napkin, fold the napkin in half and in half again. Starting with the upper right corner, roll the top layer down to the middle of the napkin (diagram 1). Repeat with the next layer (diagram 2). Tuck the rolls under to hold (diagram 3). Fold under both sides of the napkin. Tuck a Christmas ornament in the fold if desired.

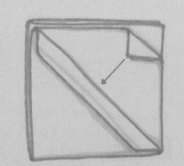

59

Bows of Gold Centerpiece

Shown on page 44

What you need

Large clear glass container such as a punch bowl
Tall goblet such as a marguerita glass
Purchased gold package bows
Purchased wrapped gold candies

What you do

Set the goblet in the center of the punch bowl. Surround the goblet with purchased gold bows. Fill the goblet with wrapped candies. Set in the center of the table.

Vintage Jeweled Ball

Shown on page 45

What you need

8-inch diameter foam ball such as Styrofoam
Black spray paint
Broken or intact vintage jewelry including pins, earrings, and bracelets
Wire cutters
Glue suitable for use on metal and plastic
Large vase or other temporary holder
Gazing ball holder for display

What you do

In a well-ventilated area, spray paint the ball black. Allow to dry. Rest the ball in the vase or holder and begin to cover the ball with vintage jewelry. If the jewelry is broken, remove any pin or backing with wire cutters before gluing to the ball. If the jewelry is intact, simply poke the pin or back into the plastic foam. Add a little drop of glue to secure if necessary. Allow to dry before moving on to another side of the ball. Cover the ball until the desired effect is achieved. Allow to dry and display on gazing ball holder.

more ideas

Embellish an artificial green wreath by hot-gluing favorite board game pieces such as checkers, chess pieces, or dice to the wreath. Add a bow and hang in the game room.

🌷

Make a "choose-a-gift" centerpiece by wrapping tiny gifts and placing them in a large bowl in the center of the table. Let everyone choose a gift for their table favor.

🌷

Paint a purchased pine cone wreath with metallic green spray paint for a stunningly simple and very sparkling holiday wreath.

🌷

Use an inexpensive rose bowl to float red and white roses with a dusting of glitter for a last-minute holiday centerpiece.

🌷

For a school room decoration for your child's teacher, get a class picture from each student. Trim and glue the pictures to a purchased wreath form and add a bow.

🌷

Top a purchased evergreen wreath with a bow tied from a vintage handkerchief. Try to find a hankie with Christmas motifs or in the colors of Christmas.

🌷

Purchase an inexpensive white fabric tablecloth. Let the children draw their favorite Christmas cookies and other holiday foods on the cloth with permanent markers or paint pens. Use the tablecloth at the children's table for the holiday meal.

Search flea markets for small chairs or stools that can be placed outside at the front door. Place a wreath or other arrangement on the chair for a warm welcome.

🌷

When serving punch, place a wreath on the table first. Place the punch bowl in the center of the wreath and arrange holly, small ornaments, and other holiday items in the fresh greens.

🌷

Mismatched crystal can combine to make a glorious impression. Collect pieces you like from flea markets, garage sales, antique shops, and second-hand or thrift shops. Set the table using the one-of-a-kind pieces.

🌷

Group white candles in a variety of clear glass and brass candleholders for an elegant centerpiece.

🌷

For a glistening centerpiece, float a poinsettia head in a large rose bowl. Place floating candles around it and light them.

🌷

Fresh flowers always add a touch of elegance to any table. For the holidays, choose red and white roses. For sparkle, touch the edges of the blooms with egg white and dust with glitter.

🌷

Make a clever centerpiece by putting one small vase inside another larger vase. Put copies of snapshots of Christmases past between the two vases. Fill the inside vase with water and add greens and fresh flowers.

christmas cookies & cakes

tasty

pretty

sweet

delicious

baked

Pretty Paisley Cookies

Use your artistic talent to create one-of-a-kind cookies that are sure to please. A spicy sugar cookie dough rolls out easily to make the little shapes. The decoration on the cookies looks sophisticated but is easily achieved using simple dots and lines. The recipe and tips for decorating these little works of art are on page 86.

Quick Wrap

Give these elegant little goodies in a square glass gift jar that has been painted with dots along the bottom to match the cookies. Tie on a paisley print paper shape for the tag.

Quick Wrap

Wrap cookies in purchased boxes that accent the colors of the frosted cookies or present them on a pretty plate in similar colors. A simple gift tag and some ribbon makes the gift complete.

Cookie Gifts

Whether you are trying to think of a gift for an avid reader, a special teacher, or an aspiring musician, you'll find that a delightfully decorated cookie is the perfect present. Make some Cookie Books, Music Note Cookies, or Apple-Shaped Cookies using the same delicious sugar cookie recipe. Then use your favorite cookie cutters to make the cookie uniquely suited for each gift. The recipe and tips for decorating are on page 87.

Retro Reindeer Cookies

Make dozens of these happy reindeer cookies that reflect upon Christmas past. Decorate them in traditional colors or use colors that were popular decades ago. The recipe and tips for decorating are on page 88.

Good Idea

Make a team of Santa's reindeer
into a Christmas garland. Simply
poke a hole in the front and
back of each reindeer cutout
before baking and then tie them
together with narrow ribbons
after they are baked.

Fancy Purse Cookies

Be your own purse designer using frosting
and all kinds of cookie embellishments.
Start with a fun purse-shaped cookie cutter
and then decorate in the style that suits you.
The recipe and tips for decorating are on
pages 88–89.

Good Idea

Keep a variety of decorative sugars and other cookie and cake embellishments on hand for last-minute decorating.

Snowflake-Topped Pumpkin Cake

Stir up a delicious pumpkin cake and decorate it using precut stencils and golden glitter dust. The easy cake is made using canned pumpkin and topped with a luscious cream cheese frosting. The decorating takes just a few minutes when you use a precut stencil and edible glitter dust. The recipe and tips for decorating are on page 89.

Quick Wrap

Make these tasty cookies in a smaller drop size and present them in a holiday mug. Add a candy cane and bow to make the gift complete.

Double Chocolate Crinkles

Santa will love to enjoy these yummy chocolate cookies with a big glass of milk on Christmas Eve. Made with baking chocolate and chocolate chips, these easy-to-make drop cookies will be a holiday favorite. The recipe is on page 91.

Lollipop Cookies

These pretty cookies will bring out the child in everyone. The cookie dough is colored, rolled, and sliced to make the clever pinwheel cookies. Arrange the cookies in a pretty box for a fun gift. The recipe and tips are on page 90.

3-D Snowflake Cookies

These stunning 3-D snowflake cookies are surprisingly easy to make. A little frosting holds the cookie shapes in place—and of course, no two are alike. Add a dusting of sanding sugar for sparkle. The recipe and instructions are on page 94.

Christmas Almond Crinkles

This simple and delicious drop cookie will be an easy addition to your Christmas cookie tray. Rolled in sugar, these tasty cookies are sure to become year-round favorites. The recipe is on page 91.

Layered Shape Cookies

Simple shapes stack up nicely to create a retro look that is a nice change of pace for the holidays. Let the kids help frost the cookies in colors that match your holiday table. The recipe and tips for decorating are on page 92.

Quick Wrap

A simple, round, brown-paper box serves as a wonderful container to hold the simple stacked shapes. Make a tag using the same shapes and colors as the cookies inside.

Peppermint Plaid Brownies

Impress your guests by making a pretty Christmas plaid in colorful frosting on an old-fashioned chocolate brownie. Just layer the frosting using different widths and colors of frosting. Recipes and step-by-step instructions for making the plaid decoration are on pages 92–93.

Quick Wrap

Purchased clear plastic take-out boxes make perfect animal cookie boxes. Carefully arrange the little cookies in the box and tie with a ribbon.

Animal Cracker Cookies

Surprise the little ones with sweet animal cookies decorated just for them. Use pastel colors and sugars to give each cookie appeal. The recipe and tips for decorating are on page 95.

Personal-Pan Chocolate Cake

Bake everyone's favorite chocolate cake in individual fluted pans for a special holiday treat. Drizzle the cakes with chocolate syrup and top with crushed peppermint. Serve with a favorite ice cream and watch the smiles all around. The recipe is on page 96.

Gingerbread Cookie Village

Purchased stencils make these gingerbread houses little works of art. Amazingly easy to do, the stencil mixture is spread on the cookies before they are baked. The recipe and tips for decorating are on pages 96–97.

Quick Wrap

Use a simple cellophane bag and pretty ribbon to tie up a single gingerbread house. Add a shiny red jingle bell to make the gift even more festive.

Pretty Paisley Cookies
Shown on pages 64–65

What you need
1 cup butter, softened
⅔ cup dark brown sugar
1 teaspoon baking powder
1 teaspoon ground cinnamon
½ teaspoon ground nutmeg
¼ teaspoon ground cardamom
⅛ teaspoon ground mace
1 egg
1 teaspoon vanilla
2 ⅔ cups all-purpose flour
1 recipe Powdered Sugar Icing
Decorating bags
Paste food coloring in desired colors

What you do
In a large mixing bowl beat together butter, brown sugar, baking powder, cinnamon, nutmeg, cardamom, and mace until light and fluffy. Add egg and vanilla. Beat until well combined. Gradually add flour and beat until combined. If necessary, cover and chill dough until easy to handle. On a lightly floured surface, roll out dough to ⅛- to ¼- inch thickness. Cut out shapes with cookie cutters (see Sources, page 159). Place 1 inch apart on lightly greased cookie sheet. Bake in 375 degree oven for 6 to 8 minutes or until edges begin to brown. Remove to wire rack to cool. When cool, frost with Powdered Sugar Icing. Makes 3 to 4 dozen cookies.

Powdered Sugar Icing: In a medium mixing bowl place 2 cups sifted powdered sugar. Add 1 tablespoon white corn syrup, 1 teaspoon vanilla, and enough milk to make an easy spreading consistency (1 to 2 tablespoons). Use a thin consistency for painting a base coat on cookies. Use a thicker consistency for piping with a decorating bag. Divide and tint icing desired colors using paste food coloring. (We used orange, teal, pink, red, and green.) For brown icing, add unsweetened cocoa powder and some additional milk.

• **To decorate Paisley Cookies:** Spread a base coat of thinned red, pink or white icing onto cookies using a clean artist's paintbrush (see photo A). Pipe dots, curlycues, and stripes onto cookies using thicker, tinted icing in decorating bags (see photo B). Let icing dry.

Cookie Gifts

Shown on pages 66–67

What you need

3 cups all-purpose flour
1 teaspoon baking powder
¼ teaspoon salt
1 cup butter, softened
1 cup granulated sugar
1 egg
2 teaspoons vanilla
3 tablespoons milk
1 recipe Meringue Icing
Decorating bags
Paste food coloring in desired colors
Sanding sugar in desired colors

What you do

In a large bowl stir together flour, baking powder, and salt. Set aside. In a mixing bowl beat butter with an electric mixer. Beat in sugar until well combined and fluffy. Beat in egg until well combined. Beat in vanilla and milk. Gradually beat in flour mixture, using a spoon if too thick for mixer. Divide dough into two portions. Wrap in plastic wrap and chill several hours or until easy to handle.

Roll out chilled dough on a lightly floured surface to about ⅛- to ¼- inch thickness. Cut out apple and music note shapes with cookie cutters (see Sources, page 159). For books, cut a 2½ x 5-inch rectangle. Fold over dough at a slight angle to make the books. Place cutouts 1 inch apart on lightly greased cookie sheet. Bake in a 375 degree oven for 6 to 8 minutes or until edges just begin to brown. Let cool on cookie sheet for 2 minutes. Remove to a wire rack to cool completely. Makes about 3 to 4 dozen cookies.

• **To decorate Cookie Gifts**: Place about ⅓ cup white Meringue Icing in a decorating bag. Twist bag shut and seal with a twist tie. Do not snip tip of bag until ready to use. Divide remaining Meringue Icing between small bowls. Tint icing desired colors with a small amount of paste food coloring. Keep icing covered when not using.

Add a few drops of water to icing colors in bowls until each is a flowing consistency. Using a small, clean artist's brush, paint the thinned icing onto cookies. Let base coating of icing dry before adding outlines. Snip a tiny opening at end of decorating bag. Pipe white icing outlines and details onto the cookies. Sprinkle with colored sanding sugar. Let dry completely (about 2 hours) before wrapping.

Meringue Icing: In a medium mixing bowl beat together 3 tablespoons meringue powder, ½ teaspoon cream of tartar, 1 teaspoon clear vanilla, and ½ cup warm water with an electric mixer. Beat in 4½ cups sifted powdered sugar on low speed until combined. Beat on high speed for about 5 minutes or until thickened and white. Makes about 3 cups.

Retro Reindeer Cookies

Shown on page 68–69

What you do

Use Paisley Cookie recipe, page 86, and cut out with reindeer cookie cutter. (See Sources, page 159.)
To decorate Reindeer Cookies: Frost baked cookie with a base coat of thinned icing. Then place some thicker, tinted icing in a decorating bag. Snip a very small opening in bag. Add outline and details to reindeer. Add silver or colored dragees and red hots to icing while still wet. Makes 3 dozen cookies.

Fancy Purse Cookies

Shown on page 70–71

What you need

3 cups all-purpose flour
1 teaspoon baking powder
¼ teaspoon salt
1 cup butter, softened
1 cup granulated sugar
1 egg
2 teaspoons vanilla
3 tablespoons milk
4-inch purse cookie cutter (see Sources, page 159)
1 recipe Meringue Icing (see page 87)
Decorating bags with coupler sets and decorating tips (round, grass
    tip #233, star)
Paste food coloring (red, pink, lavender)
Decorative sugars, edible glitter, small candies, silver dragees

What you do

In a large bowl stir together flour, baking powder and salt. Set aside. In a mixing bowl beat butter with an electric mixer. Beat in sugar until well combined and fluffy. Beat in egg until well combined. Beat in vanilla and milk. Gradually beat in flour mixture, using a spoon if too thick for mixer. Divide dough into two portions. Wrap in plastic wrap and chill several hours or until easy to handle.

   Roll out chilled dough on a lightly floured surface to about ¼-inch thickness. Cut out shapes with 4-inch purse cookie cutter. (See Sources, page 159.) Use a small sharp knife to cut out a half-circle shape below purse handle. Place cutouts 1 inch apart on lightly greased cookie sheet. Bake in a 375 degree oven for 6 to 8 minutes or until edges just begin to brown. Let cool on cookie sheet for 2 minutes. Remove to a wire rack to cool completely. Makes 1 to 2 dozen cookies.

• **To decorate Fancy Purse Cookies:** Thin about half of the icing to a syrup consistency by stirring in a few drops of water. Divide both thick and thin icings into portions to color. Add paste food coloring to make desired colors (we used red, pink, and lavender). Use the thinned icings to paint a base coat of icing onto the purse cookies using a clean artist's brush. Add sprinkles and decorative candies such as silver dragees to wet icing. Place the thick icings into decorating bags with coupler sets and decorating tips. Pipe decorations and trims onto the cookies. To make a fringe edge, place icing in a bag with a grass tip to make fringe at edges of a cookie purse (see photo A, opposite). To make roped handle, pipe icing with a star tip in a rope pattern on the handle of a purse. To make a swirled print, pull white frosting through solid frosting with a brush or toothpick (see photo B, top right).

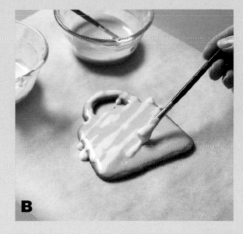

B

Snowflake-Topped Pumpkin Cake

Shown on pages 72–73

What you need

3 eggs
½ cup cooking oil
⅓ cup water
½ of a 15 oz. can pumpkin (scant 1 cup)
1 box 2-layer spice cake mix
1 recipe Cream Cheese Icing
Purchased snowflake stencils (see Sources, page 159)
Shimmer dust (see Sources, page 159)

What you do

In a large mixing bowl combine eggs, oil, water, pumpkin, and cake mix. Beat with an electric mixer on low to medium speed for 2 minutes. Pour into a greased 13x9x2-inch baking pan. Bake in a 350 degree oven for 30 to 35 minutes or until a toothpick inserted in center comes out clean. Cool on a wire rack. Frost with Cream Cheese Icing. When icing is dry to the touch, place stencil close to frosting (see photo A) and sprinkle shimmer dust through stencil (see photo B). Store cake in refrigerator. Serves 12.

A

Cream Cheese Icing: In a medium mixing bowl place 3 oz. softened cream cheese. Beat with an electric mixer for 30 seconds. Gradually beat in 1 cup sifted powdered sugar. Beat in ¼ cup milk. Add enough additional powdered sugar to make a thin frosting, about 2½ cups. Spread over cooled cake. Let icing dry.

B

Personal-Pan Chocolate Cake
Shown on page 84

What you need
3 cups all-purpose flour
2 cups sugar
6 tablespoons cocoa powder
2 teaspoons baking soda
1 teaspoon salt
2 tablespoons vinegar
2 teaspoons vanilla
½ cup butter, melted
2 cups cold water
Chocolate syrup; crushed peppermint

What you do
In a large mixing bowl mix together flour, sugar, cocoa powder, baking
soda, and salt. Make a well in the middle. Combine butter, vinegar, and
vanilla. Add to dry ingredients. Mix well. Add 2 cups cold water and beat
well. Pour into eight ungreased individual 4-inch fluted pans or two
9-inch round pans. Bake in a 350 degree oven for 15 minutes for
individual pans or 20 minutes for layers. Drizzle with chocolate syrup
and sprinkle with crushed peppermint.
Makes 8 cakes.

Stenciled Gingerbread Houses
Shown on page 85

What you need
5 ½ cups all-purpose flour
2 teaspoons ground ginger
2 teaspoons ground cinnamon
½ teaspoon ground cloves
¾ teaspoon baking soda
¼ teaspoon baking powder
1 cup butter, softened
1 cup packed dark brown sugar
1 cup light molasses
2 eggs
1 recipe Decorating Dough (see page 97)
1 recipe Meringue Icing (see page 87)
Red and green paste food coloring
House cookie cutters and stencils (see Sources, page 159)
Edible glitter, colored decorating sugar, nonpariels
     (see Sources, page 159)
96

In a large bowl stir together flour, ginger, cinnamon, cloves, baking soda, and baking powder. In another bowl beat butter with an electric mixer. Beat in brown sugar until fluffy. Beat in molasses and eggs until well combined. Gradually beat in flour mixture. Use a wooden spoon if dough is too thick for mixer.

Divide dough in half. Wrap dough in plastic wrap and chill for several hours or until easy to handle. Meanwhile, prepare Decorating Dough. Divide dough into 3 portions. Tint one portion red and another portion green using paste food coloring.

On a lightly floured surface roll out one portion of gingerbread dough to ¼-inch thickness. Cut out cookies with large house cookie cutter or trace pattern, page 98, and use as house shape. Place cutouts 1 inch apart on lightly greased cookie sheet.

• **To decorate cookies with stencils**: Start at top of a cookie and work down. Place a stencil at top of cookie and, with a small metal spatula, spread some Decorating Dough carefully over stencil, being careful not to move stencil (see photo A). Lift stencil up and wash off dough from stencil (see photo B). Pat dry. Continue with other stencils until cookie is fully decorated. If necessary, trim plastic stencils to allow you to place decorations close together.

A

Bake decorated cookies in a 375 degree oven for 8 to 10 minutes or until cookies are firm in center. Let cool for 2 to 3 minutes on cookie sheet. Remove cookies to a wire rack to cool. Repeat with remaining doughs. Makes 1 dozen cookies.

B

• **To decorate Gingerbread Houses:** Place white or tinted Meringue Icing in a decorating bag with a tip. Pipe decoration onto cookies. Sprinkle wet icing with edible glitter, colored sanding sugar, or small nonpariels. Let icing on cookie dry, about 2 hours. To store them, arrange flat in single layers with waxed paper between the layers.

Decorating Dough: In a bowl beat ¼ cup softened butter with an electric mixer. Add ¼ cup granulated sugar. Beat until combined. Beat in ½ cup light cream or half-and-half. Beat in ⅔ cup flour until smooth.

Stenciled Gingerbread House Patterns

Enlarge 200%

more ideas

Purchase small inexpensive holiday plates and large fabric Christmas-print fabric napkins at discount stores. Arrange your favorite cookies or candies on the plates. Set the plate in the center of the napkin, bring the four corners together and tie with a holiday ribbon.

❦

If frosting and decorating cookies seems too big a task this year, cut out the shapes with a cookie cutter and brush with milk before baking. Add a sprinkle of colored sugar and bake. The cookies will be easy to make and still have a lovely color after baking.

❦

Simple holiday garnishes make any recipe seem like a Christmas recipe. Use red and green holiday-shaped gumdrops to decorate a favorite cake, and red and green sugar on top of whipped toppings.

❦

Make your guests departure as warm as their arrival by giving them a few fresh-baked cookies wrapped in cellophane tied with a bow. They can enjoy your gift from the kitchen on their drive home.

❦

Surprise the kids on Christmas morning with holiday toast. Use large cookie cutters to cut shapes such as stars, bells, and stockings. Spread honey or jellies on the toast shapes to complete the fun.

❦

Add a taste of peppermint to holiday desserts by crushing up candy canes. Sprinkle over frosted brownies, cake, or vanilla ice cream.

With narrow ribbons, tie Christmas cookies and cookie cutters to evergreen swags. Hang the swags on your banister to make your stairway look holiday sweet.

❦

Make your Christmas cookies even prettier by adding a drop of red food coloring to the sugar cookie dough. The pastel pink color will add an unexpected holiday touch.

❦

Give your special homemade Christmas cookies in clever wraps. Try stacking them in a canning jar decorated with stickers, placing them in a small gift bag decorated with rubber stamping, or tying them up with ribbon in a printed paper bag.

❦

A single cookie wrapped in a parchment envelope or bag makes a great gift. Make the cookie oversized and decorate it to fit the interests or profession of the person to receive the cookie.

❦

Surprise a neighbor by baking a cake and presenting it on a pretty footed cake plate. Make the cake and cake plate the special gift.

❦

Make a Christmas cake that looks like a Christmas tree by cutting 2 square layer cakes into four triangles. Line up the triangles in a row to resemble a tree and frost with green frosting. Add round colorful candies for ornaments and sprinkle with green decorative sanding sugar.

simple

appreciated

heartwarming

thoughtful

cozy

handmade
gifts & wraps

Bead Kit Gift
Create a kit that will bring smiles to every bead lover. A small purchased tin holds the beads, wire, and findings to make a pretty little bracelet. Instructions are on page 120.

Winter Goodie Box
Clear take-out containers make perfect boxes to hold all kinds of goodies. Decorate the outside with stickers and jewels and fill the box with candy. Instructions are on page 120.

Gifted Pistachios
Give a gift of goodies and a dish to share them in. Choose a dish that shows the pretty colors of the nuts and add the jar of pistachios. Instructions are on page 121.

Bell and Holly Trim
Cut pieces of scrapbook paper into the shape of holly leaves for a simple and stunning gift wrap topper. Add gold jingle bells for the berries. Instructions and patterns are on page 122.

Jewelry Bow
A vintage pin or brooch serves as a lovely ribbon bow center. Match the paper that you use or use a contrasting piece of jewelry. Instructions are on page 122.

Curly Bow Topper
Simple pipe cleaners are curled into a bow shape to top this polka-dot package. Add some purchased pompoms to finish the colorful look. Instructions are on page 121.

Train Topper

You'll be right on track with this clever gift topper. See the kids smile when they see part of the gift on the outside of the box. Instructions are on page 122.

Toy Bow

Use leftover pieces from favorite games and toys to make a clever package topper. Use a sticker to send the holiday message. Instructions are on page 123.

Just Ducky Trim

Add a rubber ducky with a matching bow to the top of a stack of colorful striped boxes. Be sure to fill the boxes with special bath goodies. Instructions are on page 123.

Pink Tweed Crochet Hat and Purse Set

Easy to make just in time for Christmas, this derby-style hat and clutch bag are made from a pink-tweed yard. Instructions are on pages 124–125.

Pretty Beaded Necklaces

Choose beads in the styles and colors that you like and make a stunning necklace for that special person on your Christmas list. Instructions for making the necklaces are on page 126.

Quick Wrap

Present the lovely necklaces in purchased white jewelry boxes. Glitter the lid edge. Then cut a piece of scrapbook paper just the size of the lid, glue it to the top, and decorate as you wish to make a very pretty gift box.

Artist's Jar

Fill a jar with things that any budding artist will love—brushes, paints, and more. Then add a cut-paper jar topper and gift tag to complete the gift. Instructions are on page 127.

Fun-and-Games Jars

Any game-lover will appreciate a jar filled with game pieces to use all year long. Paint the tops of the jars to match the pieces. Instructions are on page 127.

110

Puzzle-Me Jar

They'll be surprised and ready for the challenge when they see puzzle pieces nicely collected in a glass jar. Be sure to add a picture of the finished puzzle so they can begin at once. Instructions are on page 128.

Sweet Cinnamon-Sugar Shaker

A purchased glass shaker can be painted and filled with sweet cinnamon sugar for a quick gift. Add a loaf of wheat bread for toasting to make a welcome and healthy gift. Instructions are on page 128.

Simple Ribbon-Ready Box

Every gift-giver will love to have a box full of ribbon all ready for gift wrapping. Fill the box with favorite colors and styles of ribbon and even a ribbon dispenser. Instructions are on page 129.

Quick Wrap

Create a quick wrap for the ribbon box by gluing pieces of ribbon to the top of the box and then clustering a group of small ornaments in the center. Add a gift tag to complete the wrap.

A Holiday Moment for Yourself

A Holiday Moment for Yourself

Step 1 Take the teacup and saucer from the bag they are in.
Step 2 Boil some water and make some tea to put into the
cup using the pretty tea bag.
Step 3 Open ... green ...
Step 4 O ... the ...
Step 5 L ... the ca ...
Step 6 C ... the co ...
Step 7 Si ... k and
think of the ...

Moment-for-Yourself Gift

Christmas is such a busy time that sometimes the best gift is a
moment for yourself. Give that gift in a clever way with pretty
essentials to make it happen. Instructions are on page 130.

114

Quick Wrap

Stack the frames and tie with a sheer wide ribbon and candy cane. It's all you need to make an already pretty gift all wrapped up.

Monogram Frames

Purchased ornate gold frames become the art that surrounds a simple wooden monogram. Simply paint the wood initial and place on the frame. Instructions are on page 129.

Blue Sweater Bag
The button front of a favorite worn
cardigan becomes the flap of a
pretty and stylish purse. Purchased
cording in the same color makes the
handle for the purse. Instructions
for making the purse are on page
131. Tips for felting wool sweaters
are on page 137.

Sweater mittens

A time-worn cardigan sweater finds a new life when it is felted and transformed into mittens with pretty trims. The mitten is cut from the sleeve of the sweater. Patterns and instructions for the mittens are on page 131. Tips for felting old sweaters are on page 137.

Gray Purse and Eyeglass Case

Choose an old sweater that has ribbing and a pocket to make this classic purse shape with handles and a matching eye-glass holder. Instructions and patterns are on pages 132–135. Tips for felting are on page 137.

Purple Sweater Purse and Tissue Holder

Don't throw that old sweater away! Instead, felt it and make a clever purse with matching accessories that will surely be treasured. Instructions and patterns are on pages 136–138. Tips for felting are on page 137.

118

Bead Kit Gift

Shown on page 102

What you need
Purchased metal tin with lid (see Sources, page 159)
Alphabet stickers
Santa sticker
Small piece of narrow ribbon
Crafts glue
Beads, findings, and wire to make one bracelet or necklace

What you do
Use the alphabet stickers to spell "Bead Kit" on the metal container.
Glue the ribbon across the lid of the box using the crafts glue. Apply
the Santa sticker to the lid over the ribbon. Fill the box with all the
beads and findings.

Winter Goodie Box

Shown on page 102

What you need
Precut snowflake stickers (available at scrapbook stores)
Purchased clear take-out box (available at crafts stores)
Tacky crafts glue
Scissors
Blue jewels
Blue sheer ribbon
Narrow ribbon for tag
Fine-tipped marking pen

What you do
Glue the snowflake stickers to the outside of the box cutting the
stickers in half at the corners if necessary. Glue the jewel to the center
of the snowflake. Allow to dry. Fill the box with candy or other items
and close. Add sheer ribbon for a handle and use one of the precut
snowflakes for a tag. Write the name on the tag and use the narrow
ribbon to attach the tag to the handle.

Gifted Pistachios

Shown on page 103

What you need
Small canning jar
Scraps of scrapbook paper
Stickers
Pistachios in the shells
Green dish
Wide sheer green ribbon
Scissors; pencil

What you do
Draw around the flat lid of the jar onto the scrapbook paper. Cut out. Add a sticker to the paper top and set aside. Fill the jar with pistachios. Place the lid flat, circle of paper, and jar ring on jar. Place the jar in the dish. Crisscross the ribbon under the dish and bring up and around the jar. Tie in a bow. Add a tag using the scraps and another sticker.

Curly Bow Topper

Shown on page 104

What you need
Wrapped package
About 10 red and green chenille stems (pipe cleaners)
Red and green small pompoms
Double-stick tape

What you do
Bend each chenille stem into two loops, like rabbit ears, bringing the ends together. Set aside. Place two or three pieces of doublestick tape on top of the wrapped box. Press the ends of each of the chenille stems into the tape with the curved ends out. Place a piece of double-stick tape on each pompom and stick to the center of the chenille stem bow. Add a gift tag if desired.

Bell and Holly Trim

Shown on page 105

What you need
Wrapped package
Small scraps of scrapbooking paper
3 gold jingle bells
Scrap of ribbon
Scissors; glue

What you do
Trace or copy patterns, right, and cut out. Draw around pattern onto scrapbook paper scraps and cut out. Glue the smaller leaf on top of the larger leaf. Set aside. Glue ribbon to top of wrapped box. Glue leaves over ribbon. Glue bells to center of box.

Holly Pattern

Full-Size Pattern

Jewelry Bow

Shown on page 105

What you need
Wrapped package
1- to 2-inch-wide ribbon
Vintage pin
Sprigs of fresh greenery

What you do
Tie ribbon around the package making a large bow. Attach the pin at the center of the bow. Tuck fresh greenery under the bow.

Train Topper

Shown on page 106

What you need
Wrapped package
¼-inch-wide ribbon with looped edges
Small train pieces
Crafts glue; scissors; paper punch
Paper and stickers for tag

What you do
Glue two rows of ribbon on top of package to resemble train tracks. Glue train parts on top of track. Punch hole in tag and spell name with stickers. Attach to package.

Toy Bow
Shown on page 106

What you need
Wrapped package or box
Old toy pieces
Small scraps of ribbon
Alphabet or word stickers
Tacky crafts glue
Scrap of paper and narrow ribbon for tag

What you do
Glue the ribbon pieces to the top of the package crisscrossing them in the middle. Arrange the toy pieces and glue over the ribbon. Place the word stickers on top of the toy pieces. Add a tag to the package.

Just Ducky Trim
Shown on page 107

What you need
Two wrapped packages or boxes
Yellow ribbon
Scissors
Small rubber duck
Tacky crafts glue

What you do
Stack the packages or boxes and tie or glue together. Make a bow from the yellow ribbon and glue to the top box. Glue the rubber duck to the top of the bow.

Pink Tweed Crochet Hat and Purse Set

Shown on page 108

SKILL LEVEL: Easy

FINISHED MEASUREMENTS

Bag: 5" tall and 18.75" around.
Hat: The hat pattern is stretchy and will fit an average
   size woman.

What you need

**Celebrity by Artful Yarns (JCA), 50g/104yd balls
(40% polyester/38% acrylic/22% nylon) ribbon**
. 2 balls for hat and 1 ball for bag in color #37
. Size I/9 (5.5 mm) crochet hook
   OR SIZE NEEDED TO OBTAIN GAUGE
. Safety pin or stitch marker
. One 1-inch-diameter button for bag

GAUGE

For bag; in sc with a double strand, 12 sts and 12 rnds
   = 4"/10cm.
For hat; rnds 1-7 = 5"/12.7cm.
TAKE TIME TO CHECK YOUR GAUGE.

What you do

BAG

Beg at the base with a double strand, ch 21. 3 sc in
second ch from hook, sc in next 18 ch, 3 sc in last ch.
Working along opposite edge, sc in 18 ch — 42 sts.
Rnd 2: (2 sc in first sc, sc in next sc, 2 sc in next sc, sc
in 18 sc) twice — 46 sts.
Rnd 3: (2 sc in first sc, sc in next 3 sc, 2 sc in next sc,
sc in next 18 sc) twice — 50 sts.
Rnd 4: [2 sc in first sc, (sc in next 2 sc, 2 sc in next sc)
twice, sc in next 18 sc] twice — 56 sts.
Body (place a marker on first st of rnd and move up
as you go)
Rnd 1: Sc in front lp of each st around.

Rnds 2-14: Sc in each sc around.
Rnd 15: Sc in each of the 56 sc around, then sc in next
3 sc.
Rnd 16: Sl st in each of next 38 sc.

Flap

Row 1: Sc in back lp of next 18 sc; turn.
Row 2: Ch 1, sk first sc, sc in next 15 sc, sk next sc, sc
in last sc — 16 sts; turn.
Row 3: Ch 1, sc in each sc across; turn.
Row 4: Ch 1, sk first sc, sc in next 13 sc, sk next sc, sc
in last sc — 14 sts; turn.
Row 5: As Row 3.
Row 6: Ch 1, sk first sc, sc in next 11 sc, sk next sc, sc
   in last sc — 12 sts; turn.
Row 7: Ch 1, sk first sc, sc in next 9 sc, sk next sc, sc in
   last sc — 10 sts; turn.
Row 8: Ch 1, sk first sc, sc in next 4 sc, ch 10, sc in
   next 3 sc, sk next sc, sc in last sc. Fasten off.

Flower

With a double strand, ch 2. 5 sc in second ch from
   hook. In each of the 5 sc (sl st, ch 5, sl st). Fasten
   off. Sew button to center of flower. Attach to
   center front of bag about 3" above lower edge and
   2" from top edge.

HAT

Rnd 1: With a single strand, ch 2, 6 sc in second ch from hook

Rnd 2: 2 sc in each sc around — 12 sts.

  NOTE: For next rnds, place a marker on first ch-sp or st of each rnd and move up as you go.

Rnd 3: (Ch 1, sc in sc) around; join with sl st in first sc — 12 sc.

Rnd 4: (Ch 2, sc in sc) around.

Rnd 5: (Ch 2, sc in sp, ch 2, sc in sc) around — 24 ch-2 sps.

Rnds 6-7: (Ch 2, sc in ch-2 sp) around.

Rnds 8-17: (Ch 3, sc in next sp) around — 24 sps.

Rnd 18: (2 hdc in each sp) around — 48 hdc.

Rnd 19: Hdc in each hdc around.

Rnd 20: 2 sc in each hdc around — 96 sts.

Rnds 21-25: Sc in each sc around. Fasten off after Rnd 25.

Flower

With a single strand, ch 2. 5 sc in second ch from hook. (Sl st, ch 7, sl st) in each sc around. Fasten off. Attach to side of hat over Rnd 18.

Crochet Abbreviations:

beg	begin(ning)(s)	rnd	round
ch	chain	RS	right side
dc	double crochet	sc	single crochet
dec	decrease	sl st	slip stitch
est	established	sp(s)	space(s)
hdc	half double crochet	st(s)	stitches
inc	increase	tog	together
lp(s)	loop(s)	tr	treble crochet
rep	repeat	WS	wrong side
rev sc	reverse single crochet		

Pretty Beaded Necklaces
Shown on page 109

What you need for both necklaces
Beading wire such as .018" 26# 12 kg
Old scissors or wire snips
Needle-nosed pliers
Necklace clasps
Crimp beads
Assortment of beads that you like
Small square of felt to arrange the beads

What you do

Cut the wire the length you want your strand to be plus 6 inches. Common necklace lengths are 13, 16, and 18 inches. Set aside. Lay out the piece of felt and arrange the beads on the felt in the order that you plan to string them. The felt will keep the beads from rolling around. Choose the type of clasp that you want to use. There are many kinds and all work well. Separate the clasp and place one piece at each end of the beads that you have on the felt. Place a crimp bead at each end of the row of beads beside the clasp piece.

Thread one end of the wire through a crimp bead, then through one end of the clasp and then back through the crimp bead leaving about ½ inch of the wire tail. Using the needle-nosed pliers, squeeze the crimp bead to keep the wire from slipping out. (What you are really doing is smashing this tiny bead.) See step 1, below.

Start stringing the beads you have laid out on the piece of felt in the order that you decided. Thread over both wires up to the crimp bead and continue to string the beads until you reach the length you like. See step 2, below. End with a crimp bead. Leave at least 4 inches of wire remaining to attach the other end of the clasp. Loop the end of the wire through the other end of the clasp and back through the crimp bead. Squeeze it with the needle-nose pliers as you did at the beginning of your strand. Feed the wire tail through at least two of the beads and cut off the excess with old scissors or wire snips. See step 3, below.

1   2   3

Artist's Jar
Shown on page 110

What you need
Quart-size canning jar with flat lid and screw ring
Scrap of scrapbooking paper
Scissors; paper punch
1 yard of narrow red cording
Paints to put in jar
Paintbrushes to put in and tie on jar

What you do
Remove the inside lid of the jar and trace around it onto the scrapbook paper. Cut out. Place the items to be given into the jar. Place the lid and screw top on the jar. Cut a rectangle from the scrapbook paper and fold for a tag. Punch a hole in the side of the tag and thread the cording through the hole.

Fun-and-Games Jars
Shown on page 110

What you need
Canning jars with zinc screw-on lids
Acrylic paint in desired colors
Paintbrushes
Game pieces, dice, poker chips, playing cards, etc. to put in jars
Ribbon
Scissors

What you do
Take the tops off of the jars. Paint with acrylic paint and allow to dry. Fill the jars with the game items. Put the lids back on the jars and add ribbon and gift tag.

Puzzle-Me Jar

Shown on page 111

What you need

Quart-size canning jar with flat lid and screw ring
Small jigsaw puzzle in cardboard box
Plastic bag
Scissors; paper punch
1 yard of sheer 1-inch-wide ribbon
Large bow

What you do

Take the lid off of the jar. Open the puzzle and place the pieces in the jar. Replace the lid. Set aside. Use the scissors to cut the smaller image from the side of the box. If there is no small image, reduce the size of the image on a scanner or copier. Punch a hole in the corner of the image. Thread the ribbon through the hole and tie onto the jar. Add the bow on top of the jar.

Sweet Cinnamon-Sugar Shaker

Shown on page 112

What you need

Tracing paper or copier
White paper; pencil
Small purchased clear glass shaker jar
Permanent glass paints in red and green
Fine-tipped paintbrushes
Red ribbon

What you do

Wash and dry the shaker jar. Be sure it is clean and dry. Referring to the photo, right, copy the lettering and holly design onto white paper with the pencil. Roll the paper and place inside the glass shaker. Use the small-tipped brush to write the words and paint the holly on the outside of the jar looking through to the pattern on the paper inside. Remove the paper. Allow the paint to dry following the paint manufacturer's instructions. Fill with cinnamon-sugar. Tie onto a loaf of bread in a bag using a red bow.

Simple Ribbon-Ready Box

Shown on page 113

What you need

Large purchased box with lid
Small purchased box with lid that fits into the larger box
Awl
Small washer
Crafts glue
Spools of ribbon in desired colors, prints, and styles to put in box
Pieces of wide ribbon for decorating large box
7 small purchased ornaments

What you do

To make the small box ribbon dispenser, use the awl to make a hole in the center of the lid of the box. Glue the washer over the hole. Allow to dry. Place a small spool of ribbon in the box and pull the ribbon through the hole. Place the dispenser in the larger box. Surround the dispenser with ribbon on spools in desired colors. Decorate the top of the big box by gluing on wide pieces of ribbon, crisscrossing the ribbon in the center. Glue the ornaments on top of the ribbon. Allow to dry. Put the lid on the box. Add a gift tag if desired.

Monogram Frames

Shown on page 115

What you need

Two ornate gold frames
Purchased wood monograms to fit on frames
Black spray paint
Crafts glue

What you do

In a well-ventilated area, spray paint the letters black. Let dry. Remove the glass from the frames. Glue the letters to the front of the frames. Let dry.

Moment-for-Yourself Gift

Shown on page 114

What you need

Large purchased box with lid
Tea cup and saucer
Pretty tea bag
2 purchased or homemade cookies
Cellophane wraps for cookies and teacup/saucer
Small votive candle and holder
Small box or bag to hold candle and holder
Printed note with instructions
4 x 5½-inch piece of pink cardstock cut with decorative scissors
Narrow sheer ribbon
Paper punch
Pink tissue paper

What you do

Copy or print the note, below. Cut out. Glue to the piece of scrapbook paper. Punch a hole in the corner and add a piece of ribbon. Place the cookie in the bag and tie with ribbon. Use tissue paper to pack all of the items in the large box. Put lid on box. Add a ribbon bow if desired.

A Holiday Moment for Yourself

Step 1   Take a teacup and saucer from the bag they are in.
Step 2   Boil some water and make some tea to put into the cup using the pretty tea bag.
Step 3   Open the box and take out the glass votive holder.
Step 4   Open the candle and put it into the votive holder.
Step 5   Light the candle.
Step 6   Open the cookies and take one out.
Step 7   Sit back and relax, sip your tea, enjoy the cookie, and think of the blessings of this most wonderful time of year.

Sweater Mittens and Bag
Shown on pages 116–117

What you need for the mittens
Tracing paper or copier
Preshrunk felted wool sweater with ribbed sleeves (see felting tips, page 137)
White paper; pins; matching thread; scissors

What you do for the mittens
Enlarge and trace or copy mitten pattern, bottom right. Lay mitten pattern with pattern straight edge opening just above the ribbing edge of preshrunk sweater sleeve, (see photo A). Cut out pattern through both layers of sleeve, with cut side edges easing into seam of circular ribbing. With right sides together, stitch around sides and curved edges, using ¼ inch seam allowance. Ease side edge stitching into existing ribbing side edges. Clip carefully in center of thumb curve. Turn right side out. Fold cuff up or leave down for longer warmth. Decorate with small circles and remaining buttons cut from front of sweater, ¼-inch trim for bows, or as desired.

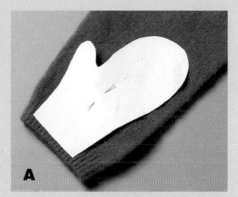

A

What you need for the purse
Tracing paper to make cut paper pattern rectangle to accomodate sweater type and measurement
Preshrunk felted wool sweater with front button closure (see felting tips, page 137)
39 inches of ¼-inch-wide decorative cording
Buttons from sweater front opening
Pins; matching thread; scissors

What you do for the purse
Make a rectangle paper pattern to accommodate sweater type, planning the pattern to cut sweater across fabric front button opening to form top overlap of purse. (Purse shown folds over to a finished size of 5½ x 8½ inches. Paper pattern was 11 x 9 inches.) Unbutton placket. Fold up bottom about 5 inches with right sides together. Insert cording handle at top side edges. Backstitch over cording to secure and continue sewing around side and bottom edge in a ¼-inch seam. Clip corners and turn right side out.

↑ ✕
**Place just above
bottom of sweater
ribbing**

**Sweater Mitten
Pattern**

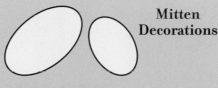

**Mitten
Decorations**

Enlarge 200%

Enlarge 200%

Gray Purse and Eyeglass Case
Shown on page 118

Shown on page 118

What you need for the purse
Tracing paper or copier
Preshrunk wool sweater with pocket (see felting tips, page 137)
One 1-inch coat button
Buttonhole thread
Purchased purse handles (6½ inches wide x 4¾ inches high)
**Scrap from plaid shirt flannel or ⅓ yard of flannel fabric to match
     sweater/purse color**
⅓ yard medium weight iron-on interfacing
Matching thread; pins; scissors

What you do for the purse
Enlarge and trace or copy patterns, pages 134–135. Cut purse pattern
from bottom of sweater fabric, having top straight edge of pattern
aligned along bottom ribbing edge, with the ribbing extending beyond
the straight edge of the pattern. Cut one purse pattern from the front of
the sweater and one from the back of the sweater. Slit open the sleeves
of the sweater, iron the piece flat, and cut two outside pocket pieces with
the straight top edge of the pocket at the edge of the sleeve ribbing. Trim
the neckline ribbing from the sweater to be used as the loop closure.
Cut lining pieces from a recycled flannel shirt or other flannel fabric.
Cut 2 purse body pieces from iron-on interfacing, cutting interfacing
even with top fold line marked on pattern.

Iron interfacing to the back of the flannel lining pieces. For the
lining pockets, iron ½-inch seam to the back of side and bottom edges;
clip curved edges. Fold and iron top edge of lining pocket ¼-inch
and another ½-inch under. Topstitch pocket top along folded edge
to hem. Place wrong side of lining pocket to right side of lining purse
pieces, placing in center of purse, 2 inches down from top fold line.
Stitch pockets close to folded side and bottom edges, reinforcing at tip
corners. With right sides together, stitch purse lining pieces together
at side and bottom edges, starting at point indicated on pattern. Clip
curves. Narrowly hem remaining open side edges.

Sew sweater pockets to front sweater fabric, placing at center and
1¾ inches from bottom edge. Stitch close to cut edges, reinforcing at
top corners. (There is no need to fold under raw edges since the felted
wool doesn't ravel.) With right sides together, stitch a ¼-inch seam
on the side and lower edges of purse, starting and stopping at points
indicated by an X on the pattern.

Make a depth tuck (dart) in both lining and sweater fabrics as indicated on the pattern forming the darts with right sides together. Trim sweater seams to ¼ inch. Do not trim lining seams. Flip the lining darts up.

Make loop closure from 7-inch ribbing taken from neckline of sweater. With wrong sides in, fold length together to make strip about ¾-inch wide. Fold strip in half and insert between lining and purse at center of one side at the top, cut ends extending down into the seam allowance. Insert lining into purse, with wrong sides together. Pin top and side edges, placing fold of lining at purse fold line. Sew lining to purse, stitching close to side edges and across fold line.

Insert handles by folding top ribbing edge through handles and lapping over to purse front. Pin through both layers, forming a casing for handles. Stitch through all layers, just above ribbing edge, gathering purse together to slide along handles as you sew across the bag. Sew large coat button to the side opposite the loop closure, using buttonhole thread to secure button. Trim ribbing at side edges, fold seam under and hand stitch the ribbing together at side edges.

What you need for the eyeglass case
Tracing paper or copier
Scrap of preshrunk wool sweater
One ⅞-inch black button
Buttonhole thread
Black embroidery floss
Scissors; matching thread

What you do for the eyeglass case
Enlarge and trace or copy pattern, page 135. With wrong sides together, fold bottom straight edge up to top corners of rectangular shape. Sew around outside edges, using 3 strands embroidery floss. Sew buttonhole stitch from bottom right corner through both layers of fabric to top flap. Stitch around single layer of flap and around left side through both layers. Make a small slit for buttonhole at center of flap. Stitch small buttonhole stitches around slit to reinforce opening. Sew button to purse bottom directly behind buttonhole.

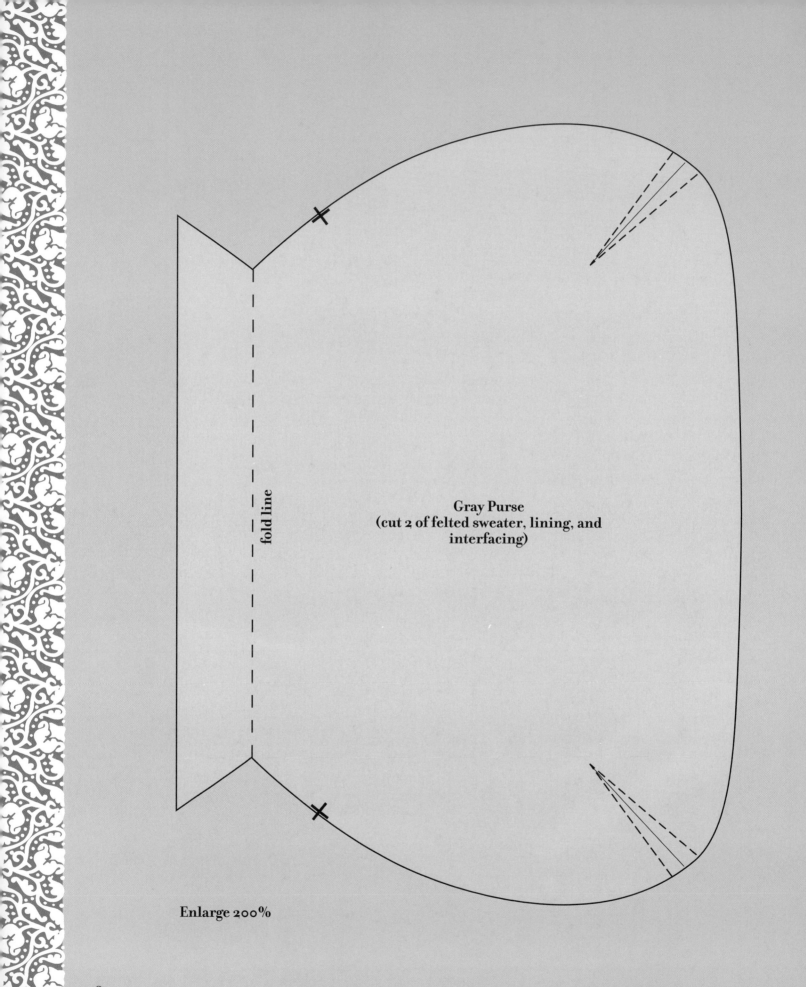

fold line

**Gray Purse
(cut 2 of felted sweater, lining, and
interfacing)**

Enlarge 200%

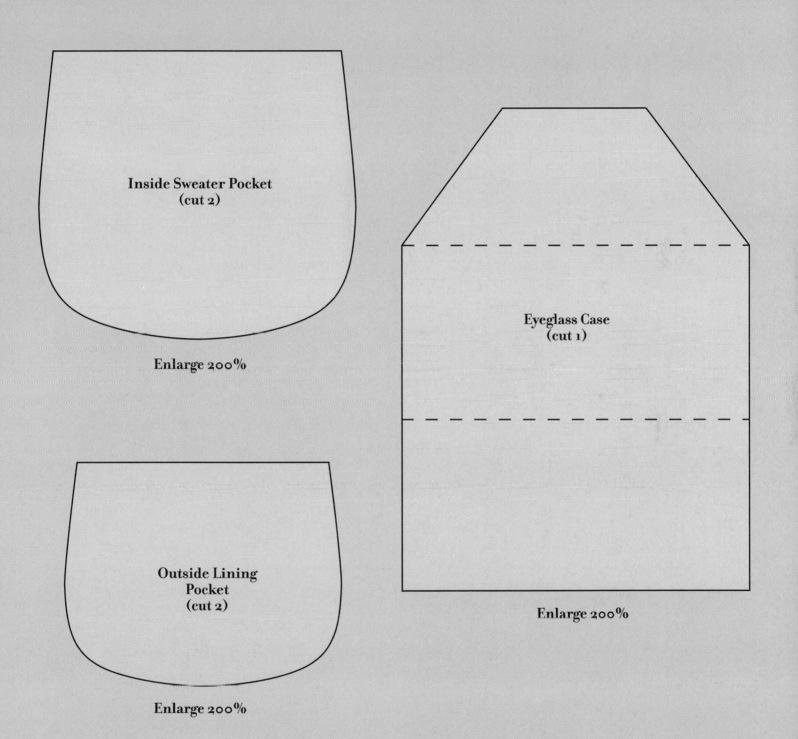

Inside Sweater Pocket
(cut 2)

Enlarge 200%

Outside Lining
Pocket
(cut 2)

Enlarge 200%

Eyeglass Case
(cut 1)

Enlarge 200%

Purple Purse and Tissue Holder
shown on page 119

shown on page 119

What you need for the purse
Tracing paper or copier
Preshrunk felted sweater
64 inches of ⅜ inch-cording, cut into two 32-inch lengths
½ yard of ¼-inch cording, cut into two 9 inch lengths
Matching thread
¼ yard heavy weight iron-on interfacing
¼ yard lining fabric

What you do:

Enlarge purse pattern, page 138, and cut out. Cut purse pieces from sweater bottom, having top straight edge of pattern aligned with the bottom of the sweater so that the ribbing extends beyond the straight edge. Cut handles from straight grain of remaining sweater fabric, piecing if needed to make two strips 1½ x 32 inches long and two strips ¾ x 8 inches long. Cut pocket from sweater front or make one from sweater fabric, using pocket pattern piece.

Iron interfacing to wrong sides of purse sweater fabric. With right sides together, sew side and lower edges of purse, starting and stopping at side edges at the point where the sweater ribbing begins. Use a ¼-inch seam allowance. Clip curves and turn right side out. With wrong sides together, sew remaining side edges of ribbing on purse. Fold ribbing edge to outside of purse.

Edgestitch pocket piece to the center of one right side of lining piece, about 1 ½ inches from top straight edge. With wrong sides together, stitch side and lower edges of lining pieces together, using ¼-inch seam. Fold top edge of lining ½ inch to wrong side and iron flat.

Fold each ¾ x 8-inch strip of fabric around the ¼-inch cording. Using matching thread, hand stitch long cut edges together around cording. Fold one wrapped cord in half to make a loop and baste place at center top of back of purse, having cut edges extend ¾ inches into purse from top fold edge of ribbing. With other wrapped narrow cord, tie a loose knot in center as a clasp. Fold in half and baste in place at opposite top edge of purse.

Wrap each 32 inch length of ⅜-inch cording with sweater fabric and hand sew long cut edges and each short end of strips. On outside of purse front and back, make small holes to insert handles by clipping slits ¼-inch wide and ⅜-inch long at points marked on pattern, making sure this spot is just under the sweater cuff folded over. Tack the clipped pieces to the backside by taking a few hand stitches.

Tie loose knot in one end of each handle. Insert long straight end of each handle through a hole from the front side of purse then from back side to the outside on the remaining hole. Tie another loose knot near end of handle. Insert other handle through purse in the same manner. Pin handles to purse at top edges and baste in place at top folded edge, keeping ribbing free. Put lining inside purse, with wrong side of lining facing wrong side of purse. Edgestitch around top edge at fold line, through handles, loop and knot clasp, laying ribbing out flat. Fold ribbing down to outside of purse to finish.

136

What you need for the tissue holder
Tracing paper or copier
8x8-inch piece of felted wool
Matching thread; scissors; decorative yarn (optional)

What you do
Enlarge pattern, page 138, and cut out. Trace onto piece of felted wool and cut out. With right sides together fold long edges together to fold piece in thirds. Overlap long edges ½ inch to make rectangle 3 ¼ x 6 inches. Stitch ¼-inch seam on short sides. Clip corners to reduce bulk and turn right side out. If tissue holder opening is cut across the grain and is stretchy, reinforce the edge of the overlapping flap by hand stitching decorative yarn around the straight edge.

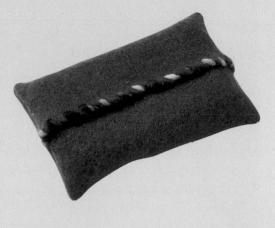

Tips for Felting Wool Sweaters

- Choose sweaters with 100% wool fiber content, or as much wool as possible for best shrinkage. Sweaters containing angora rabbit hair also shrink and felt well.
- Wash sweaters in very hot water with a small amount of laundry soap. Agitation of the washing machine helps to loosen the fibers and shrink the wool. Placing sweaters inside old pillowcases during the wash will save your washer and drains from clogging up with the thousands of tiny fibers that wash out of the sweaters.
- Dry sweaters in very hot dryer to shrink and felt the item the maximum amount.
- To keep from stretching the fabric out of shape when sewing by machine, try using an even-feed or walking foot attachment. It is also helpful to lengthen the stitch slightly and lighten the pressure placed on the presser foot of the sewing machine.
- Tightly felted wool does not ravel and edges and seams can usually be left raw or unfinished similar to regular felt.

- If wool fabric shrinks up so dense and thick that it is hard to sew by machine, handstitch pieces together and use pretty yarns for a special decorative effect. Even thick, dense wool is fairly easy to pull yarn through.
- When choosing sweaters to recycle and determining projects to make, look closely at the individual design elements of the original sweater for inspiration in making projects. For example, button front openings add nice details for edgings on scarves or flaps of purses. And save every button for trim details on mittens or purses. Wide bottom ribbing edges are great for hat bottoms. Wide ribbing neck edges of sweaters could provide openings for a drawstring purse. Ribbed edges of sleeves are perfect for mitten cuffs.
- Use your imagination, letting the colors, designs, and details from the original sweater determine the overall look of your felted project.

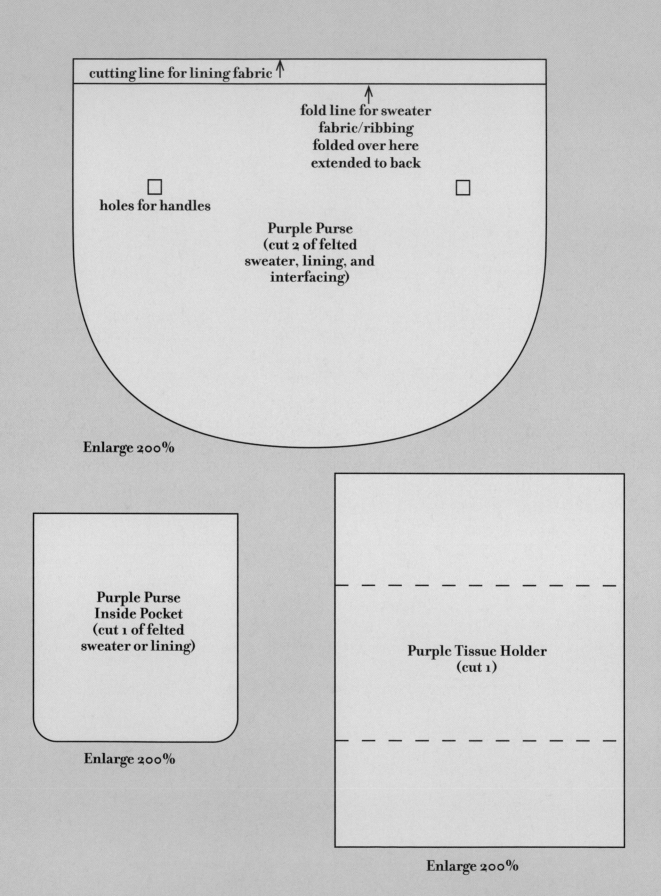

cutting line for lining fabric ↑

fold line for sweater
fabric/ribbing
folded over here
extended to back

holes for handles

**Purple Purse
(cut 2 of felted
sweater, lining, and
interfacing)**

Enlarge 200%

**Purple Purse
Inside Pocket
(cut 1 of felted
sweater or lining)**

Enlarge 200%

**Purple Tissue Holder
(cut 1)**

Enlarge 200%

138

more ideas

Fruit baskets make great gifts. This year add little goodies to the basket to make it extra special. Add favorite candies, colorful bottles of soda, playing cards, or unique kitchen utensils to personalize the gifts.

Use the fronts of old Christmas cards to cut into puzzle pieces. Put the individual pieces into a colorful envelope and take the project along for a "something to do" little gift for the kids while you drive to the mall to go Christmas shopping.

Make every wrapped package special by attaching a special trinket to the bow to personalize the gift. Try using wrapped candies, ornaments, toys, jewelry, or other unique items to add an unexpected twist.

When mailing holiday gifts, be sure to use appropriate packing and boxes. If you do not have them on hand, take your gifts to a mailing store and they will do it for you. Many catalog companies will mail your gifts directly for you at no extra cost.

Remember thoughtful neighbors at Christmas time with a small, meaningful gift. Some ideas are a homemade certificate for free snow shoveling, fresh baked bread, or a pretty holiday plant.

Express your appreciation to people who make your life easier throughout the year. Give small gifts to your mail deliverer, hair stylist, co-workers, and other special people you want to thank.

When guests will be staying overnight, surprise them with a basket of goodies left on their beds or in the bathroom. Select items such as shampoo, soap, cotton balls, hand lotion, and toothpaste.

For the seamstress on your gift list, fill a canning jar with sewing supplies. Choose items such as a colorful tape measure, embroidery floss, needles, scissors, spools of thread, or beautiful buttons. Put the flat on the jar and cover with a circle of cross-stitch fabric. Screw the lid over the flat and add a colorful tag and a bright ribbon.

Go to the movie theater and buy an empty popcorn box. Fill the box with a favorite DVD, a bag of microwave popcorn, seasoning salt, special candies, and napkins. Add a tag that says, "Join me for a movie?"

Brighten up the holidays for the family pet by personalizing his dog dish. Use sponges to cut letters that spell pooch's name and stamp on the outside of his bowl.

holiday
paper fun

personalized

delightful

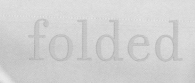

folded

printed

textured

Cash Cards

Everyone loves to get money for Christmas. This year tuck some cash in a special handmade holder and place on the tree. These little money holders are quick to make using two-sided scrapbook papers. Instructions for making the money holder cards are on page 150.

Santa Claus Cards

Make Santa the star attraction when you have him take center stage in these easy-to-make pop-out cards. Use double-sided tape to add some glittery bricks for the chimney. Instructions and diagrams are on page 151.

Star-Punched-in-Pink Card

A purchased star paper punch is the secret to making a clever see-through card with a greeting inside. Add a pretty brad and floss closure to complete the pretty card. Instructions are on page 150.

Pretty Ribbon-Trimmed Cards

Rubber stamp your favorite message and then add purchased stickers and a piece of your favorite ribbon. So easy to make, these cards can be sent to everyone on your Christmas list. Instructions are on page 151.

Mini Stickered Cards

So little and sweet, these cards can be used as Christmas greetings or gift tags. Just use sticker alphabet letters and holiday motifs on tiny purchased cards. Instructions are on page 152.

BAKING SPIRITS BRIGHT

YUM!

This holiday season, our kitchen was filled with Bailey's kitchen goodies. So yummy!

May your holidays be merry & bright!

HO HO HO

Baking Spirits Bright

Create a scrapbook layout to tell your story of holiday baking, complete with photos and recipes. Use the scraps you have leftover from your layout to make a clever Ho Ho Ho Card. Instructions for both projects are on pages 152—153.

Winter Wonderland Christmas

A scrapbook layout can be very simple and striking to look at by using the negative space to advantage. Create a simple page and use the leftover scraps to make a Warmest of Wishes Card. Instructions for both projects are on page 154.

The True Gifts of Christmas

Make some Christmas memories by creating a scrapbooking layout using favorite photos. Then make a Noel Card by using the leftover scraps of paper and embellishments. Instructions are on pages 155–156.

Cash Cards
Shown on page 142

What you need
7 x 7-inch square of two-sided scrapbook paper
    (see Sources, page 159)
Crafts glue
One large sticker
Paper punch
¼-inch-wide ribbon

What you do
Lay the paper square on the table turning the paper so it looks like a diamond with a point at the top. Bring the bottom point up and fold to within 1-inch from the top corner. Fold the left side in, just past the center. Fold the right side in over the left side. Secure with crafts glue. Add a sticker to the front of the card. Punch a hole in the top of the card and place the ribbon in the hole for hanging. Place money in the pocket.

Star-Punched-in-Pink Card
Shown on page 144

What you need
Purchased pink tri-fold card and envelope
Star-motif paper punch
Coordinating printed paper for inside of card
1 x 3-inch piece of white vellum
Pink fine-tip permanent marker
3-inch piece of pink embroidery floss
¼-inch decorative brad
2 large stickers
Scissors; glue stick

What you do
Use the paper punch to make star punches on the front flaps of the card. Cut a piece of matching coordinating paper to fit on the inside of the card. Write "Merry Christmas" on the white vellum and glue to the inside paper. Poke the brad into the left front flap of the card and open the back prongs. Glue the piece of embroidery floss in a loop and glue to the other side for a closure. Add a sticker to the card front. Place another sticker on the envelope flap.

Santa Claus Cards
Shown on page 143

What you need

7 x 7-inch piece of red or gold vellum or lightweight paper
Scissors
Pencil
Double-stick tape
Fine glitter in desired color
Large Santa sticker

What you do

Fold the paper in quarters, referring to step 1, below. Open up one fold and with the fold at the left, mark and A and B in the top and bottom corners, see step 2, below. Referring to Diagram A, make two cuts on the folded edge. Open up the card, see step 3. Fold the top (A) to the back. Pop out the cut section, see step 4. Turn the card vertically so the pop-up section comes out the front. Cut the double-stick tape into small rectangles and place on the top of the card to resemble bricks. Peel off the tape front and dust with glitter. Add the large Santa sticker to the front of the pop-up card.

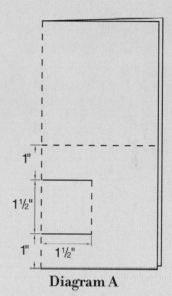

1"
1½"
1" 1½"

Diagram A

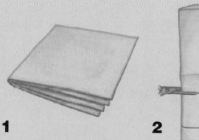

1

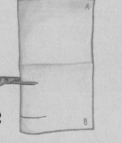

2

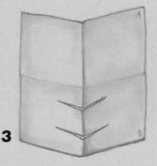

3

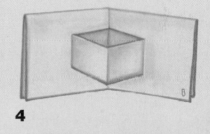

4

Pretty Ribbon-Trimmed Cards
Shown on page 145

What you need

Purchased teal blue blank greeting cards
Rubber stamp with Christmas greeting
Red ink pad; fine red glitter
Small round and square stickers
Small pieces of 1-inch-wide printed ribbon
Clear crafts glue

What you do

Stamp the greeting using the rubber stamp and ink pad. Dust with glitter. Let dry. Glue the ribbon to the edge or top of the card. Add the stickers where desired.

Mini Stickered Cards

Shown on page 146

What you need

**Small purchased cards with parchment envelopes
(see Sources, page 159)**
Ruler; pencil
Small size silver alphabet stickers
Small 3-D stickers such as stars, birds, etc.

What you do

Decide what saying you want to put on the cards. Using a ruler, make a light line where the alphabet stickers are to be placed to spell the words. Carefully place the letters to spell the message. Add the 3-D stickers to the cards. Add additional stickers to the envelope front where desired.

Baking Spirits Bright

Shown on page 147

What you need

White and green 12 x 12-inch cardstock
Striped and patterned paper
Coaster tags
Die-cut letters
Ink such as Colorbox Fluid Chalk
Acrylic paint
Brads
Ribbon
Chipboard
Corner rounder
Sandpaper

What you do

Create the layout on a 12 x 12-inch piece of white cardstock. Cut a 6 x 12-inch strip of green cardstock. Ink the edges and adhere to bottom half of white sheet. Cut a 3x12-inch strip of patterned paper. Sand edges to reveal white core; adhere along top edge of green strip. Using reverse side of cardstock, cut a narrow strip of cardstock, sand and adhere along bottom of striped paper.

Place a 4 x 4-inch photo in the space directly above the striped paper, approximately ¼-inch from the right edge of page. Customize a tab with "Yum" (typed, stamped or handwritten) and adhere to 4 x 4-inch photo using matching brads. Keeping margins consistent, adhere a 5 x 7-inch focal point photo to the layout, about ¼-inch from the edge of the 4 x 4-inch photo and overlapping the striped paper.

Adhere a 2½ x 2½-inch photo directly below the 5 x 7-inch photo, aligning right edges. To make your own chipboard accent: Cut a 3 x 3-inch piece of chipboard and round the corners. Cut a 3 x 3-inch piece of patterned paper. Round the corners and adhere to chipboard. Sand edges. Adhere chipboard accent directly above 5 x 7-inch photo, aligning right edges. Customize the chipboard tag by inserting brads over some of the Christmas ornaments. Instead of inserting brads into the 4 corner holes provided, thread ribbon through 2 holes at bottom and tape to back of tag. Tie ribbon through top 2 holes, adding a second color before finishing knot. Sand, adhere, and ink premade chipboard accents and adhere next to 2½ x 2½-inch photo, keeping margins consistent. Use die-cut, sticker, or rub-on letters to create the title. To add interest, cut a strip of yellow cardstock, round corners, ink, and use it as a base for "Spirits". Finish the layout by adding photo corners to upper left and lower right corners.

Ho Ho Ho Card

Note: Use your leftover materials from the scrapbook layout to make a holiday card.

From leftover green cardstock, cut a 4¼ x 11-inch rectangle. Score and fold in half so that card opens at bottom. Round corners and ink edges. Use die-cut, sticker, or rub-on letters to create "Ho Ho Ho" along the front bottom edge of card.

Cut a 4¼ x 2½-inch strip of white cardstock and adhere across center front of card, directly above writing. From leftover patterned paper, cut a narrow yellow strip and adhere across top edge of white cardstock. Cut a narrow strip of "happy holidays" print and adhere across bottom edge of white cardstock. Use a pre-made chipboard circle (or cut your own). Use paint or marker to color the edges of the chipboard, if visible. Trace the chipboard circle onto the back of the striped patterned paper. Cut out the circle and adhere to the chipboard. Sand edges. Adhere striped ornament to card. Use a die cut or sticker letter to make an ornament hook. Cut a small piece of patterned paper for the base of the hook. Tie a narrow ribbon and adhere with a glue dot. Punch small circles and adhere across white cardstock as desired.

Cut a 3¼ x 4½-inch piece of white cardstock and adhere to inside. Add a strip of patterned paper and a greeting.

Winter Wonderland Christmas

Shown on page 148

What you need

White and blue cardstock
Die-cut snowflake stickers
Acrylic letter stamps
White ink such as Colorbox Fluid Chalk
Brads
Ribbon
Circle punches (2 sizes)
Paper piercing tool
Wave trimmer
Paper lacquer such as Crystal Lacquer

What you do

Create layout on white cardstock. Begin by trimming and placing photos. Place largest photo (5 x 7-inch) to left side of layout. Trim additional photos to fit in a grid at right, keeping margins consistent. Adhere photos with lower edges approximately 4 inches from bottom of layout. Use a wave trimmer to cut strips from two shades of light blue cardstock (or draw a pencil line and cut by hand).

Adhere the darker strip below the photos with the wavy edge downward. Cut a ¼-inch strip of the same color and adhere it above the top edge of the photos. Then adhere the lighter wavy strip, wavy edge upward, overlapping the darker strip.

Using small, acrylic letter stamps, carefully stamp "Snow" in white ink across the bottom edge of the lower wavy strip. Leave space between words to accommodate brads. Continue stamping edge to edge. Use a paper piercer to make holes between the stamped words. Insert brads through layout.

• **To make the title:** Cut a chipboard mat the same size as the title sticker; adhere sticker to mat. Ink the edges in white. Carefully apply paper lacquer to center portion of snowflake and let dry for several hours, preferably overnight, following manufacturer's instructions. When dry, adhere to lower right portion of layout.

• **To make snowflake embellishments:** While the round snowflake stickers are still on backing, carefully apply paper lacquer and let dry. Punch cardstock circles in white/blue to coordinate with stickers. Punch chipboard circle as a base. When snowflakes are dry, adhere them to the matted punched circles and chipboard. Then adhere to layout along the top curve.

Warmest of Wishes card

Note: Use your leftover materials from the scrapbook layout to make a holiday card.

Trim a piece of white cardstock to 4¼ x 11-inches. Score and fold in half so that card opens at right side. Carefully use a wavy trimmer (or cut by hand) to cut a wave from the top portion of the card front. Cut the wave portion free with scissors. Cut a piece of light blue cardstock to fit inside card, then cut a wave across the top edge of it. Ink in white and adhere to inside of card. Apply border sticker across bottom of card front.

Add a "mitten weather" sticker to lower right portion of card front. Type or stamp in dark blue "warmest of wishes" on white cardstock, cut out and apply to inside of card. Add snowflake sticker above the greeting. With card closed, punch a hole along the right edge of card, through front and back. Insert eyelets if desired.

Tie a ribbon through the holes. If using two ribbons (wide and narrow), thread the ribbon through the holes at the same time and tie both pieces together.

The True Gifts of Christmas

Shown on page 149

What you need

Pink and pink/grid print double-sided cardstock
Holly patterned cardstock
Plastic letters
Ink such as Colorbox Fluid Chalk
Brads
Ribbon; strong adhesive
Circle punches
Computer
Fine black marker

What you do

Create layout on pink/grid pattern side of double-sided cardstock. Ink edges of cardstock in dark pink.

Cut a piece of holly pattern cardstock to measure 11 x 9-inches and place lengthwise across the pink cardstock, ½-inch from bottom edge and flush with right side of page. Choose 2 pieces of coordinating pink ribbon, including a 14-inch-length of wide pink ribbon. Tie a narrower piece of ribbon around the wide ribbon and knot toward the left side. Use strong adhesive to adhere the ribbon across the top edge of the holly paper. Wrap ribbon around layout and tape to back. Print photos in black and white if colors are distracting. Ink edges of all photos in white.

Adhere a 5 x 7-inch photo to top right corner of page. Slip a piece of pink cardstock (inked and cut to fit) below the 5 x 7-inch photo. Place flush with right side of page, leaving space for journaling.

Adhere a 4 x 6-inch photo to bottom left area of page, flush with the 5 x 7-inch photo. Adhere two smaller photos (2 x 2 and 2 ½ x 2 ½) in the area above and below the two larger photos.

• **To make the title:** Print "the true" on glossy photo paper and punch around text; ink in pink. Mat with a larger circle punched from a darker color and insert pink brad into top of circle to resemble tag. Adhere to page, above ribbon bow. Adhere self-adhesive plastic letters "gift" using the lines on the grid paper for spacing.

• **To make the center accent:** Create a text box on a computer. Insert a symbol or dingbat snowflake. Change text color to white, then fill the text box with a color to match the paper. Print out, punch around snowflake, ink and adhere to a larger white punched circle. Adhere the accent at the point where the photos meet.

• **To make the bottom title block:** Print out "of Christmas" and journaling strips on glossy photo paper. Cut around, ink, and adhere to layout. Use pink brads to accent journaling. Cut out holly leaves from leftover paper. Adhere to bottom corner of layout, using dimensional dots if desired to add dimension.

Noel card

Note: Use your leftover materials from the scrapbook layout to make a holiday card.

Cut a 4 x 8-inch piece of white cardstock; score and fold in half to open at the bottom. Ink around edges of card in pink. Cut a 2 x 3-inch strip of holly paper; ink and adhere to lower left hand portion of card. Cut a 2 x 1-inch piece of darker paper; ink and adhere to remaining space at bottom of card. Cut a ½ x 4-inch strip of pink cardstock; ink and adhere to card. Tie leftover ribbon around strip of cardstock to align with the seam between paper sections; adhere to card. Center and adhere plastic letters "noel" to top portion of card.

Cut a 3 x 3-inch piece of leftover pink cardstock. Adhere to inside of folded card. Write "wishing you the joys of the season"with fine black marking pen.

more ideas

Create a card that features your child's original artwork. Let your child draw on a piece of 4x6-inch cardstock using crayons or markers. After the art is completed, glue it to a folded card with a 5x7-inch front. Embellish around the edges with a bit of rubber stamping or tiny colored buttons.

Old photos make wonderful images on the front of greeting cards. Color-copy the photos and adhere to the front of a folded piece of cardstock. Don't be afraid to use the ones that feature you as a teenager!

Make a keepsake card by embellishing the front of the card with a small piece of cross-stitch that you have created. Fringe the edges before you attach it to the front of the card. Sign and date the card.

Purchase a simple greeting card and make it your own by adding a bit of glue and glitter to solid areas of color.

To make a clever card for giving money, use decorative scissors to cut off the top of a small colored envelope. Decorate the envelope with metallic markers. Glue it to the front of your blank card. Fold the money and slide it inside the envelope pocket.

Let the kids help make the Christmas cards this year. Using a rubber-stamp ink pad, have each child design a card using fingerprints. Then add lines and designs with a fine-line marker.

Make your family photo the focus of your greeting card this year. Have the photo taken in black and white and have everyone wear solid light-colored clothing. Using colored pencils, color in areas or draw tiny holiday prints on the plain light areas of the photo. Mount the photo on black paper and attach it to the front of the card.

To display the holiday greeting cards you receive, use a paper punch to make a hole in a corner and use ribbon to attach the cards to holiday greenery atop a mantel or down an indoor railing.

When mailing holiday cards, choose holiday stickers or sealing wax to place on the back of the envelopes for an extra special touch.

Keep Christmas cards from year to year to recycle. Snip portions for gift tags or decoupage onto gift boxes for colorful holiday containers.

Create a small Christmas recipe scrapbook. Design each layout with a favorite holiday recipe and a photo of the person that created the festive dish. Be sure and journal about this special person.

Keep an assortment of Christmas scrapbook papers on hand for making last-minute greeting cards and gift tags.

index

sources

Adhesives
Quick Grip Beacon Adhesives
125 MacQuesten Parkway South
Mount Vernon, NY 10550
914-699-3400

Beading Supplies
Michaels Arts and Crafts
1-800-michaels
www.michaels.com

Candy Canes
www.bobscandies.com

Cookie Cutters, Cookie Cutter Sets, and Cookie and Cake Decorating Supplies
Sweet Celebrations
1-800-328-6722
www.sweetc.com

Crafting Adhesive Tapes
ArtAccentz
Provo Craft
Spanish Fork, Utah 84660
www.provocraft.com

Fabric Stabilizer/Pellon
6932 SW Macadam Ave Suite A
Portland, Oregon 97219
1-866-333-4463
www.createforless.com

Flowers (wreath)
Creative Coop. Inc.
Memphis, Tennessee 38118

Greeting Card Blanks/Envelopes
Pure Paper
Windsor Heights, Iowa 50311
515-255-3533
www.pure-paper.com

Metal Tin Container
Pure Paper
Windsor Heights, Iowa 50311
515-255-3533
www.pure-paper.com

Peppermint Chips
Andes Peppermint Crunch
www.tootsie.com

Scrapbook Papers
Holiday Paper Squares
Brave Ink Press
515-964-1777
www.braveink.com

Scrapbooking Ink
Colorbox Fluid Chalk
www.stampstruck.com

acknowledgements

Lyne Neymeyer (book design)
Lyne has designed dozens of books for various leading publishers across the country including Better Homes and Gardens® books. She has also taught book design at the university level and brings a fresh and creative approach to every book she designs. A photographer as well as a designer, Lyne's talents are many—as evidenced in the varied and appropriate styles she is able to create in her work.

Jennifer Peterson (food artist)
Jennifer has the unusual talent for making her decorated food into beautiful artwork. Her work can be seen in cooking magazines and books throughout the country including Better Homes and Gardens® magazines and books, and Cuisine at Home® magazine.

Dean Tanner (photographer)
A talented food and crafts photographer, Dean Tanner of Primary Image is best known for having a great eye for composition and color in his work. His work can be seen in various books and magazines across the country including Better Homes and Gardens® magazines and books, and Cuisine at Home® magazine.

And the angel said to them, "Be not afraid; for behold I bring you good news of great joy which will come to all the people; for to you is born this day in the city of David a Savior, who is Christ the Lord."

Luke 2: 10-11